The Greatest Companion:
Reflections on Life, Love, and
Marriage After Sixty

Large
Print

The *Greatest Companion*

Reflections on Life, Love, and Marriage After Sixty

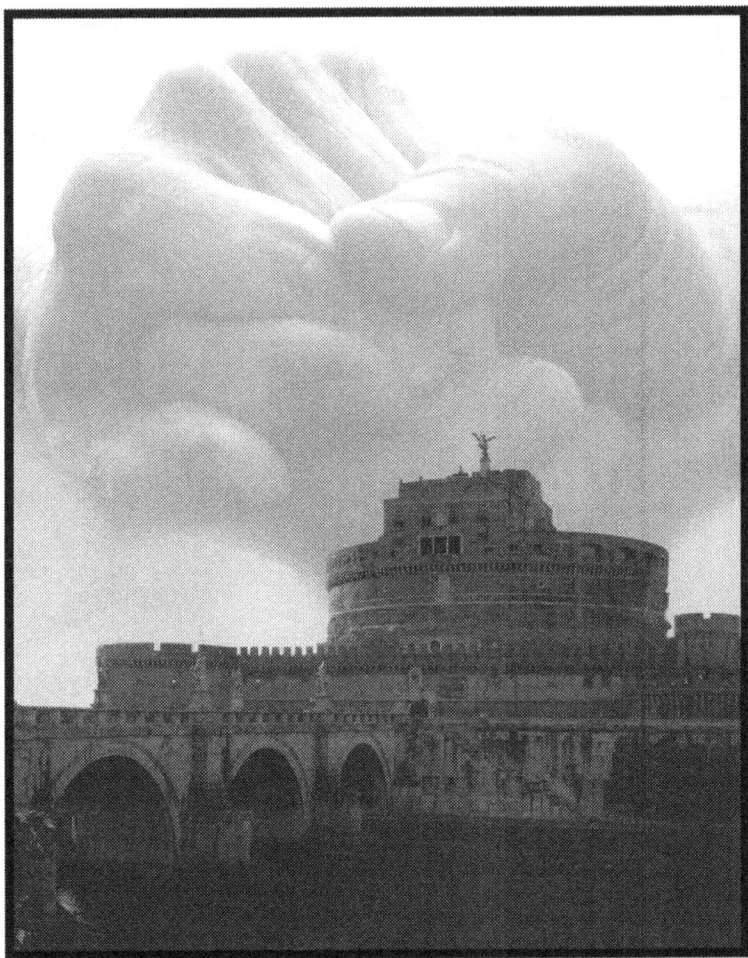

ROBERT WOLLEY

Author of "Seniors in Love"

Hatala Geroproducts • Greentop, Missouri

Acknowledgement

Do you find her attractive?
    She's very pretty.
Is she beautiful?
    I don't know.
Don't know or won't say?
    Don't know.
You can say; you won't hurt my feelings.
    She's very pretty.
Prettier than I?
    Not as beautiful as you.
Double talk. Pretty, beautiful? What's the difference?
    There is a difference, my dear. My heart tells me you
    are beautiful. Fair of face and form, yes; you know
    I find you so. But within, that's where beauty begins.
    You are beautiful because I love you.
I don't believe you, but for the moment I'll believe your
                                                    heart.

    Then I am beautiful, too?
Well, let's not push this too far.

Alas, I wasn't found to be beautiful, or even worthy.

        Good times cannot be recaptured,
        only memories blithely unmasked;
        bad times cannot be amended,
        only forgiveness given and asked.

Published in the United States of America
by Hatala Geroproducts, Greentop MO 63546 (pop 427)
09 08 07 06 05   1 2 3 4 5

The Greatest Companion: Reflections on Life, Love and
Marriage After Sixty by Robert Wolley

ISBN-13: 978-1-933167-43-5
LCCN: 2006938241

Prose and poetry celebrating
the joy of late-in-life love,
reminders of what such a love
needs to flourish, and reflections
upon love's end.

Cover Design: Shaun Hoffeditz
Cover Photo: Mark Hatala
Interior Illustrations: Twila Schofield
Composition: Age Positive Editorial Services

Table of Contents

Introduction and Excuses

You'd think giving a book a title would be easy. Just find some words or a phrase to describe the contents and you have it. Were that so in this instance. When I wrote *Seniors in Love*, the title evolved naturally, although it was not the original working title. As I worked on that book, I kept asking myself what I was doing, and the answer, "writing about seniors in love," maintained my focus and eventually become the title.

The original title for *Seniors* was my poem, "The Steps of Love," which gave the book its outline and from which I took chapter headings. This book's working title was another poem title, but that didn't work; it was too cute and humorous and forecast eventual sadness. I had to do better.

I toyed with the word "marginalia," the thought notes one writes in the margins, and a number of other weird and bizarre words, disproving, as I think about it, all theories about intelligent life in the seventh decade. I remembered something Oscar Wilde wrote: "Be warned in time, James, and remain, as I do, incomprehensible: to be great is to be misunderstood."

I'd like to be great; that's an ordinary human wish; but certainly I don't want to be incomprehensible and/or misunderstood.

Complicating the search for this book's title was the fact that half of the book is in prose and the other half in poetic form(s). I worked with such titles as "The Prose and Poetry Book for Seniors in Love." Very bad, and other ideas were worse, as you can imagine. Finally I settled on *The Greatest Companion: Reflections on Life, Love, and Marriage After Sixty*. That describes the purpose, content and orientation of the book.

* * *

Seniors was written especially for those who had reached or had gone beyond the magic age of sixty and who, as its subtitle, "A Second Chance," suggests, were dealing with the many issues of an older person discovering and holding onto a new life partner following separation (e.g., death, divorce) from a former partner.

Having used the word, there really is nothing magic about age sixty, only that in its wisdom the government has decided to base many of its census figures on that age. Statistically, officially, when you and I get to sixty, we're considered old, and once the government gets it into its head that age sixty is the magic boundary, we're stuck in the realm of the aged.

It's all quite arbitrary and archaic, and in fact, chronological age has relatively little to do with being old and absolutely nothing to do with being "over the hill" and certainly nothing to do with being in love.

I live in a neighborhood of single family homes, most occupied by retired people. There are more children than there used to be; properties turn over more often than in multiage neighborhoods. Disability and death are common among the retired. Gradually, our neighborhood is becoming multiaged, and I take quiet delight in the squeals of laughter and exuberance when my neighbor's two tiny children play in their front yard.

Anyway, a woman neighbor said to me the other day, "I wonder if it's healthy living in a neighborhood of all old people."

She's ten years older than I, but I knew what she meant. I look at my neighbors, and some days I worry because they have become old and frail. Thank God, I tell myself, I'm not old like that.

Then I go to the local sandwich shop for lunch, pay the bill, and note that without asking, the young woman behind the counter has given me a senior citizen's discount. She sees what I don't, even when I look in the mirror.

I wonder just when I became old. I try to remember and I cannot. Honest. Was it when I got married? When the first child was born? When I made my first investment in a mutual fund, planning for my children's education (and lost it all in one of our depressions)? When I took out a health policy and a life insurance policy? When my children were growing up and I suddenly realized my own mother would have died had she known some of the things I did as a child? Was it when my oldest child began to date? Or when the children went off to college? Or when the first grandchild came along? When I first drew Social Security checks? When my wife died? When bum knees and torn shoulders took my golf handicap out of single digits and into duffer's territory? Honest. I don't know when I ceased being young and became old.

Okay, my hair is gray, my face wrinkled, my limp noticeable, my step slower than it was. That's the physical appearance. The lunch counter clerk saw that. What she didn't see is that I still play golf without embarrassing myself too much, that I still sail with the best of sailors, that I work on my books four or five hours each day and maintain a work ethic of long standing, that I just remodeled the downstairs of my house, new bedroom and new bath, the house I built with my own hands when I was fifty-three. That took exactly three hundred and sixty five days from the day I began clearing the lot to the day my late wife cooked a turkey in the new oven. Twelve or sixteen hours every day with only three days off during that year. I'll admit it: my new downstairs took three months, and there was a lot of resting, plenty of resting if the work was particularly strenuous. I realize just how old the body has become.

Yet I don't define my age by the extreme physical efforts I no longer can accomplish. I have no speed/distance records to set, no unclimbed heights to conquer, no endurance masterpieces to achieve. There are plenty of personal, individual accomplishments left, but they are personal, not universal challenges.

What's left are matters of the heart and mind. When I was young, the horizon was a distant image. Now it's within sight--and there is so much to do and to accomplish before, finally, I fall over the ultimate edge.

I know I voice the thoughts of many older people when I claim that our life's unfinished business is mental and spiritual. and as regards the purpose of this volume and of *Seniors in Love*, the spiritual includes the ageless need to give and to receive love.

* * *

The Greatest Companion presents its ideas in two ways: a series of thought pieces and a collection of poems. The poetry, love poetry by my definition, sometimes but not always relates to the prose both in this book and in *Seniors*, and lest you feel cheated, one prose piece does not have an accompanying poem or poems.

* * *

The Prose:

The informal prose pieces more or less speak for themselves. The name for a formal thought piece is "essay," from French and Latin roots, *essai* from sixteenth century French meaning attempt, and *exagium*, Latin for try or examine. Dr. Johnson of eighteenth century dictionary fame called the essay "an irregular or undigested piece" of writing. I hope that is not your judgment. As a prose form, the essay has come a long way since Johnson's pejorative judgment two hundred and fifty years ago. Today an essay usually is a formal presentation of intellectual and philosophical thought.

The formal essay style is not how I wish to present the prose portions of this book. My prose pieces are somewhere between the "irregular and undigested" and the formal thought. To use a more contemporary expression, I'm "having a go" at certain ideas that reflect upon and expand ideas originally presented in *Seniors* or ideas that were not explored.

"Essay" is too formal a word and "thought piece" is too egoistic; "commentary" is close but not on the mark. As I write I'm stuck with "thought piece." If I come up with a better idea, I'll use it. If not, we're both stuck with it and I'll beg your forgiveness because I couldn't find a satisfactory synonym.

I reject the essay's implied concept of formalism because I want to keep thoughts simple, in words that are understandable. There are millions of essays printed in one forum or another. I take my cue from Hal Borland and E.B. White and Gore Vidal and others like them who wrote or write of great and profound and universal themes with simple words: nature, human behavior, politics, values. If my thoughts have no value, a fancy vocabulary isn't going to help them. The only formality I will attempt to observe is to write in a reasonable grammatical style, and I do that in order to understand what I have written and so you have a chance to understand what you read.

Rejecting the formal essay, I reject also the use of the royal "we." There is nothing we-ish about my thoughts in these pages. I am responsible for them, both the prose and the poetry; it is I who wrote them and I who cannot hide behind a collective pronoun, glancing toward someone else who might be made to take the blame.

Sometime I do use "we," when I believe I am speaking

for us all, but even then I don't seek your agreement (actually, that's a little white lie) with everything. That would be contrary to human nature. I seek your reflection upon and your consideration of the points raised. I try not to give outright advice. Since I don't know you and you don't know me, advice wouldn't be very reliable.

You will come to know me better than I know you; that's an unavoidable risk I take. I take the risk because a part of what I am and have experienced is universal and common to most human beings. We (see, I do use the word) fall in love and hope we will be loved in return. We dream and hope our dreams will come true. We seek a partner (wife, husband, mate) and hope to find one who will be with us forever. Sometimes we are disappointed, and it's the pain that lasts. Most have been there. Sometimes we lose because of forces beyond our control. Most have experienced that, too. Dealing with human emotions, we admit the mysteries of why we feel as we do. For all that love is, it is a journey into the unknown, and that alone places us all on common ground.

* * *

The Poetry:

Gaius Valerius Cutullus was a Roman poet in the century before the common era. He wrote love poems, many to a woman who was married to one of Julius Caesar's henchmen. Cutullus must have led a charmed life. Most of Cutullus's letters were in poetic forms, too. One letter to Varus contained his judgment about Suffenus, another Roman poet: "...A man brighter than diamonds / or what (if anything) is even more polished, / becomes less clever than the least clever rustic / when he turns to verse."

The polished part we'll ignore; it's the bad verse (not meant to be clever but least clever nonetheless) that worries the poet. To chance being regarded as "the least" because of bad poetry is a great risk of one's ego.

A while back I purchased a used copy of *Selected Poems*. In one of the margins someone had written, "Poetry works on you before you understand it." The poem was T.S. Eliot's "The Love Song of J. Alfred Prufrock," the man who was unable to love. Prufrock wonders "Do I dare? and, Do I dare?" love, that is. "Do I dare / Disturb the universe? / ...there is time." And then almost immediately one of Eliot's most quoted lines, "I have measured out my life with coffee spoons." Prufrock is growing old; there is someone to love, but he doesn't dare to risk love, even knowing there isn't time, because he fears rejection and distrusts love. "... in short, I was afraid." The waste.

Or take a contrary example, Elizabeth Barrett Browning, she of that era called "romantic," the 1800's.

First, I have to clear up the "romantic" part. Carried over from the previous century, Western civilization was engaged in a ideological war of ideas and attitudes: romanticism vs. rationality, emotion vs. pragmatism, the subjective vs. the objective, faith vs. science. Those named in the following paragraphs represent both sides of the arguments. Of course, as suited their needs, they frequently cross over the dividing line, Keats, for instance, writing rationally about basic emotions or Monet painting subjectively with great objective precision. However, for a time the romantics won out and framed the age in subjective emotionalism based on a faith in the ultimate goodness of the human being.

Without assigning sides, it was the poetic age of Wordsworth, Scott, Coleridge, Moore, Gordon (Lord Byron), Shelley, Keats, Sands (Amandine Aurore Lucile Dupin), Longfellow, Whittier, Alfred, Tennyson, the Brownings, George Elliot (Marian Evans Cross), Whitman, and Emily Dickinson among other poets.

In art, it was the age of Manet, Millet, Monet, Catlin, Cézanne, Pissarro, Sargent, Seurat, Sisley, Bierstadt. In literature, Harte, Dana, Twain (Samuel Clemens), Tolstoy, Flaubert, Cooper, Emerson, Melville, Harriet Beecher Stowe, Thackeray, Poe, Emile and Charlotte Brontë.

It was a time of great political upheaval, shortly after revolutions in France and America. The age included the terrible Civil War in America and the emancipation of Italy from Austria, France and Spain. Yet, also, it was a time of bursting creativity throughout most of the world, the United States' Civil War not withstanding. All those writers and artists, plus Rimsky-Korsakov setting music free from traditional forms and Johann Strauss giving music romance. And Elizabeth Barrett Browning could write,

> How do I love thee? Let me count the ways,
> I love thee to the depth and breadth and height
> My mind can reach....
> I love thee with the breath,
> Smiles, tears of all my life - and if God chooses,
> I shall but love thee better after death.

Such lines are condemned today as so much sentimental slop. So are Strauss waltzes in some circles, and Cooper's wilderness heroes and Manet's landscapes and Scott's poetic images.

Elizabeth Barrett was a sickly, over-protected child. She and Robert Browning fell in love through their correspondence and eloped after a secret romance, much to the distress of her stern and bleak father. The couple fled to Italy where they were married. Elizabeth became well, because of Florence's climate some say, because she was freed from her terrible father others say, because of Robert's love she said.

At the time Robert and Elizabeth "discovered" each other, she was one of England's most popular poets; he was, perhaps, England's least read poet, published but ignored. When the couple ran off to Italy, something wonderful happened. Each provided a spark for the other, igniting gigantic bursts of poetic creativity. Robert now is considered a major romantic poet, sometimes hard to read, always worth the effort. Elizabeth is considered a minor poet, the lines above most often quoted. In familiarity they lose the depth and intensity of the feelings that produced them.

When Robert wrote, he spoke his feelings through a marvelous array of characters: a musician, a painter, an old man, a nobleman, a madman. Not Elizabeth. She spoke straight from her heart. Her "Songs from the Portuguese," the Portuguese part her unsuccessful attempt to make you think they originated elsewhere, are from her heart, her love for her husband, intimate and personal. The "Songs" moved readers when they were published (1850) and for years have done so. But there were (and are) those critics who say the songs are too personal, too intimate and never should have been read by people other than Robert.

I wonder. The Brownings' love story is too precious to waste, and I'm a sucker for creative love stories. It ended with Elizabeth's premature death. Robert's last book was published on the very day of his death. Two people in love, through their love, elevated each other to dramatic heights. If Elizabeth had not revealed her feelings, would we have known either? What they, like all masterful poets, brought to their readers was a breadth of personal experience, not only real to them but made real for whomever read their lines. In the days when both Brownings were well considered, a fine movie was made of Elizabeth's life, "The Barretts of Wimpole Street" (1930).

10

* * *

Writers in whatever genre are concerned with life, its victories and its tragedies. Some of the themes are familiar; some are mysterious; all are fascinating; all are vital. Love is one such theme, in success and in failure.

I debated a long time with myself about this collection, especially the poetry. Did I want to share everything that is here?

As regards the poetry, the answer is no, yet if I didn't, was I being honest, with you and with myself? If you're going to see one side of love, you should should see the other. Those poets I most appreciate did that; I will not equal their quality but at least I can achieve their honesty.

Unlocking the True

Love unlocks
the truth in you,
the truth in me.
Who are you,
who am I,
love asks, willing
to risk what truth
might reveal,
that behind
our shields we hide
uncertainty.
"I'm no king;
a peon."
"Nor I a queen;
far from it."
White lies can't
hide the truth:
we're nobodies;
nobody,
that's for sure,
nobody 'til
a love unlocks
what is true: we
are more. Love
makes common
uncommon,
turns nobodies
into grand,
glorious
real live monarchs.
That's the truth,
as you know.

A New Ship and the Light to Sail Her By

Stout ships are launched with grand promise:
no matter how high the seas,
they will prevail against all storms.
Great ships sail toward endless horizons,
the unmarked arc beckoning,
itself a promise that there, just beyond sight,
will be revealed a land and a time
in which orchids grow and happiness reigns.

Once we sailed on such hopeful ships
and looked toward the unblemished horizon.
Some completed the journey, some did not.
The shipwrecked looked in awe, saw with envy
those who do and blamed fate or the gods or luck
- or themselves - for failure of ship and crew.
Ships do sink, crews do fail, storms prevail
and only flotsam and jetsam remains
of the high hope and once giddy crew.

Worst are those who sailed in ghost ships,
aimlessly drifting in rudderless crafts
filled with shattered dreams and soulless crew.
We might have jumped ship, did not;
we might have abandoned ship, did not.
Choosing to remain, we became ghost-like,
devoid of hope, our survival somewhere
over the darkly clouded horizon.

Then, not by our choosing or hand,
our lifeless ships grounded,
and freed of martinet command,
we stepped ashore.

Some will never sail again, the dreary
passage binding their feet to the safer shore;
some will think no second chance, no ship will call
or wish to risk a once-failed crew
whose sea bag fills with guilt and fear.

I stood thus in pain and hurt, angry that I
could not undo the done, fix the broken, right the
                                                wrong,
calm the waves, hold back the storm, save the ship,
save myself. If only.... The fault I took as mine.
If only I.... and long raged an inner storm of guilt
for my failure (which was not mine alone).

Mistakes I made; I guard against making more.
I'll not repeat the mistakes of before
(make new ones, perhaps), but one mistake
I nearly made, that to sail no more.
Was easily said with no ship in sight
or crew to sail her with,
but there, coming into view....
Do I hail her should she sail alone?

I've jettisoned my inner storms,
consigned them to the deep;
I've wiggled my toes in the sand;
I'm free to leave the shore.
I think now I could sail a ship,
her hand and mine upon the helm,
sail true the desired course,
and if past storms reappear
and hurt and fear persist,
no match they for crew of two
whose hands steer straight and true.

Love Speaks in Silence

I

I hear your words;
I do not hear your soul.
In silence is truth,
for in silence do two souls
speak. Words are precious,
yet so eloquent
they are bound by meanings.
A word means one thing to you;
to me, perhaps, something else.
Thus silence without words
conveys messages of the heart
only another heart hears.
Silence speaks through the eyes,
through the touch of a hand,
with the nod of the head,
through a smile or a frown.
I hear your words
and am glad for them.
I would hear your soul
and rejoice.

II

To hear the sound of love we must be quiet;
without silence there is no knowledge;
there is a rhapsody of truth in stillness.
Between words, between laughter, between sighs,
there is a heartbeat heard only in silence.
Words tell us much, but it's the heartbeat

that reveals all truths.
No matter where we are, on the edge of truck filled streets,
amid the clatter of saws and hammers,
riding the clang-clanging rails of a train,
next to the reverberating thrust of jet engines,
in the noisy city, in the midst of verbal disagreements,
there is silence and stillness, and it tells us
all we need to know.
Above the hustle, above the competing noisy confusion,
could I place your hand upon my heart,
you'd feel the silent rhythm of love.
My hand upon yours, feeling your pulse,
tells me all I need to hear, speaks quietly
of what we hold dear. In silence
we speak our love.

In the Middle of the Night

She doesn't know or has never said
she knows -- sometimes love words are unspoken --
there are times in the middle of the night
I'll awake, reassured that in our bed
she's there. Sound asleep, she's not aware
I'm looking at her. The temptation
to touch her repressed -- she doesn't like that,
startling her in sleep -- the carnal urge
repressed, still I look, the wonder of her
filling my head. I ask myself if she's real
and hope she's dreaming of me and us.
My whole life's there beside me,
present, future. I release a sigh.
How I long to feel and speak, tell her,
in the middle of the night, woman,
you are my world, my spirit, my breath.
In the dark of night, you are my light;
in the blistering sunlight of day,
you are my shade; in the ebony
of doubt, you are my truth; in pain,
my comfort; in joy, my compatriot.
All that she knows. What she doesn't know
is that silently in night's darkness
I reaffirm my love for her. Then
I sleep, love dreams refreshed to keep.

Oh, That I Could Give You Wings

Oh, that I could give you wings to fly uplifted
above the mundane earth and frothy sea,
or if not wings, then spirit free of doubt and fear,
or if not wings, then the voice of winged birds,
you to sing free from the highest branches above
the fallow ground in which I sow in toil
the seed that does not grow.

Oh, how I want for you a life above my own,
the touch of golden sun that melts the heart,
the rainbow's apex, and at each end, pots of gold.
If not these nor wings to fly, then such love
that in your heart all things you dream are possible
and you might say, "I am loved, life's richness
mine." That, I tried to sow.

On Lovebirds and Mockingbirds

Some words thoughts out leap,
so bear with me as I write
of feathery thoughts,
the heart/love sound of cousin
birds that sweetly sing.

Listen to lovebirds:
from their throats the purist sound;
improvised love words
flow sure and profound. For whom
are notes intended,
bride, bridegroom, for all to hear?
All, of that I'm sure,
oratorio to life,
awe and happiness,
and to mate, the eloquent
songs of love, love notes
sung for him or her alone.

Listen carefully
to the false voiced mockingbird
singing lies carte blanche,
songs learned but not its own. No!
Love does not copy
or imitate do, ra, me,
echo other's love song
melodies. Sweet they are
but fake, not self found.
Shun counterfeit mockingbirds;
if love is to be sung,
make the delicious sounds your own.

I would be the carolist singing
heartbeat rhythms of my own,
for mate alone, prose transposed
into evensong and day song profound.
I would have that voice
and sing my songs a cappella, soli,
or in chorus, the solo
me, the chorus we.
I sing to you, for you, my love.
Sing your songs back to me;
sing we then our harmonious duet
for all the world to hear.

Stout Ships and We Who Sail Them

Aye, the ships we sail, many seas they've seen,
     and storms. Some nearly floundered once or twice,
but stout ships they are and long have been,
     their compass true, and sails as white as snow.
Aged adventurers we, with expectant gleam of youth
                       in eye and heart.
     outward bound again, far horizons yet to go.

Old? For us the word's unknown.
Wiser than youth, wiser and eager,
     sturdier, more sure, tried in trial.
It's true: hulls of green heart and stout oak
     age well with use, have proved their strength,
     and if a check or crack, well, mark the trials
                     that tested the best.
Ah, yes, there go the painted ladies of the sea,
and the gleaming gents, weak hulled but pretty,
     both home bound
         because the sea's too rough and tumble,
     their ships too frail,
         all speed and glitter.
Sure, we'd like to look like that,
     no scars, no wear.
We'd be the painted lady, the dandy gent just once but can't.
     We are what we are,
         worn, scratched, tried and true.

We've voyages yet, hulls down, wind in our teeth,
                 rigging singing get up and go.
Hoist the main, the jib, the mizzen.
Hold the wheel steady as she goes,
     let gnarled but honest hands guide her tenderly.
See how she slips through the waves;
     let painted ladies and dandy gents see her strength
                and they who sail her;

let us tell of storms subdued;
let them listen and wish the same,
      sitting in placid harbors, ice in their drinks,
        land locked secure, and unfulfilled.

Where have the good men and women gone?
    Gone to sea in craft tiny and large,
    gone to seek new meanings for old lives,
    gone to sea beyond the shore
       before the sea and shore are no more.
Some sail alone, some with mate,
    all seeking life before fate
       sounds a last, mournful horn
       or clangs one final channel bell.
Sit on the verandah and rock
or guide faithful ship and mock
    old age and painful joints.
The landlubber, the doubter, they who do not dare
    sit and stare at far horizon, deny its pull,
while the risk-taker, the believer, the bold
    wonders what's there and goes off to see.
El Dorado? Avalon? The Fountain of Youth?
None, perhaps. Those are young folks' dreams,
       and there they sit, dreaming pleasure
    while the old folks search, strive,
       reach, knowing what the young do not:
dreams come true only for those who dare
    and risk all to find them.
Perhaps there is a Camelot somewhere;
    maybe a prince or princess awaits.
Who knows? But this we know:
    not to go to sea signals our end.
So, up the sails, cast off, set the course,
    be away to rainbow's end.

The Fabric of Our Lives

I've heard the phrase "the fabric of our lives" many times but don't know its origin, somewhere in antiquity.

One of my professors used the phrase frequently. The fabric of this or that was made up of threads, the warp and woof, meaning the longitudinal and right angle cords that are part of every idea and every action. Rachel Carson wrote about the "fabric of life," meaning our interdependence with all things and the relationship of all things to us.

I don't use the phrase much; it's become hackneyed and trite with overuse. Its contemporary replacement is "the web of life," and that's becoming tiresome, too.

But the truth of both phrases is permanent. Our lives may be likened to an afghan or a tapestry, to a fishing net or a spider's web. Countless threads go up and down, back and forth, the knowledge, experiences and influences that have become the tapestry of our lives, what we were, what we are and what we yet will become.

Some of those threads were twisted before we were born, our genes. Some were twisted in our earliest days and later, environment and our place in history and society. Some were threads provided by parents and siblings and friends. Some threads were gold, some were lead, the good and the bad influences that helped make us what we are. Some important threads we recognized at the time; some we came to recognize only later. Some threads are of our own making; some came from sources and forces beyond our control.

All those threads are woven into what we call the ego, the intricate web of our individual, unique self.

Carson, surely not the originator of the idea, was

correct. Life is a web-like fabric, and many of the individual threads which make up our single fabric are attached to other fabrics, and they and ours to still others, on and on, back into time, across the wide present and on into the future.

To help my students understand the nature of words, I used to lead them in an exercise to determine the meaning of their names. I would explain that "woll," the first four letters of my last name, came from England where it meant "wall," as in wall maker, or Scotland where it meant "wool," someone who worked with sheep and wool. Or the first three letters of my family name went back to England where "wol" had to do with wolves. No, I didn't know whether we hunted them, were afraid of them, or were raised by them. Yes, maybe it was like in Rome with.... Romeo? Of Rome.

Anne, Matthew, Thomas: saints. Jesus, Mary, Joseph, Mohammed, Grace? Religious names. Blanche, Read, White, Black, all colors.

Such Anglo-Saxon names as Carpenter, Miller, Shepherd, Mason were obvious. When people had only one name, Robertson was the son of Robert; Dejohn was the son of John; MacPherson was the grandson of Pherson who was the son of.... You get the idea. Then the Italian, Spanish, Germanic, Asian names. Of course I was in over my head, saved only by "naming" books.

Ask your parents. Every name has a history, is part of a larger fabric, and in most cultures one's name is the most important thing with them.

And then ask or find out why names beginning with "Mac" or "de" or "O" or "La" excluded girl children. "Deborah Robertson" is a contradiction of sorts if she is not the daughter of Robert's son. "Peggy O'Neil," too. It was all in fun and the students enjoyed themselves. And they did consider the lesson that every word is of importance. I had one student going in circles for a time. His last name was Lane. I suggested it had French origins, LaNee, meaning "the earlier or before one," not, probably the truth, the path on which some ancestor had lived. Fortunately, he had a great sense of humor and so did his parents.

Why does a wife take her husband's name? Why doesn't he take hers? Why are horses referred to as "out of?" No one wants to be know as "sired by" whomever. But humans were, once, until sire became a generic term for the head guy of an estate or town, or kingdom. Words and their meanings. Look it up. "Oh, Mr. W.!" But it happened, not always but often enough to make an impression. Words and what they mean are important. They connect us. Names connect us; we have a history. Respect each other's name.

Names are words, therefore, like names, the words we speak are important. Chose them carefully; make each word work for you, not against you. Words are tools. The best workman usually has the best tools. (More about certain words elsewhere.) And so it went in the classroom and so it is in life. Words are the verbal threads of our lives.

But once again I've digressed. Our names tell something about our beginning, little about who or what we are or how we are connected. That awareness comes from within ourselves.

If, and I'm sure you've paid attention to the lesson, two people, two mostly separate fabrics, are joined, as certainly would be the case with two people in love, then much of their individual fabrics have to be knitted together. It's only natural. With the binding of separate fabrics is created a third and new fabric.

The old threads are there; they are all that has gone before, history and biology, relationships and experiences. Some threads are precious memories, some are not so precious, may even be extremely unpleasant. Yet they're all a part of what we are.

Now, coming together with someone new, we have two tasks: to weave what each is into a common fabric, twisting together the brightest and strongest cords of two lives, and from those new threads to weave a brand new fabric. Whether one is the warp or the woof is of no concern; there's no way of telling if the weaving is shared. Each contributes to the tapestry or the web until a new cloth enwraps both.

There will be untied threads, loose ends. Love will help you deal with them. They are important but not as important as the knots you and your loved one tie with and for each other.

I've never been to a ceremony of marriage or union in which someone has not pointed out, correctly, that the couple is embarked on establishing a new and unique partnership, that each brings past history and traditions and experiences--and fresh hopes and expectations--to the union, and that henceforth they are joined in creating, for themselves, a fabric of life which will be different and new. It's not how they weave as much as it is that they must weave their separate threads together into a cloth that is both their security blanket and their safety net, the threads of which bind them together, not as a leash but as lifelines, not as tethers but as silken cords sent out ahead into the future, pulling them into the unknown but secure in the knowledge that each has spun in truth and trust and that what they have created is, like a masterful Persian rug, both functional and beautiful.

Might Have Been

Back then under rainbow's gleam
when nothing seemed too far,
we might have climbed the rainbow
or caught a shooting star.

The mind said stay;
the heart said go;
one answered yea,
the other no.

Torn between land and sky, we
let the multicolors dim,
and so today what might be
becomes what might have been.

A New York Moment

Outside Madison Square Garden,
the theater part,
before the graduation affair
of NYU,
amid the pressing hustle of
the ten thousand
self-assured, self occupied
families and friends,
two stood alone, unsure, lost in
foreign New York.

Their child's life was to commence;
they came to see
and celebrate hard work, sacrifice,
accomplishments.
Crowded New York intimidates
and bewilders
the uninitiated.
Where do we go?
How find our daughter/son?
That in a glance.

Then a sublime human moment.
She looked at him
with all the trust and faith reserved
for small children.
Adoration, "whither thou goest...."
I wanted to scream
at him, "Look at her! You'll never see
such love again."
I wanted to say I'd give my soul

for the beauty
of that look, the unconditional love,
unreserved faith.

He didn't look. In their moment of utter chaos,
she had offered
her mate her whole being, her trust
and her belief
in him. Unaware, missing his own commencement,
he led her deeper into the crowd.

Puzzlement

Perhaps I speak too often,
should leave the thoughts unsaid,
create mystery, doubt,
uncertainty, a vacuum.

Maybe I don't speak enough,
say the deep loving words
that reassure, heart sounds
of passion and continued love.

Too much or too little? Will
she tire of one, wonder
the lack of the other?
Love doesn't know the balance.

K.I.S.S.

Okay, you know KISS without the points (periods) as an acronym for "keep it simple, stupid."

Not that either of us is stupid, but not keeping things simple often is stupid. There are those who would go so far as to say that the less simple (or the more complicated), the more stupid something becomes.

Medicine and its many related procedures is very complicated, yet I've listened in as physicians or surgeons have explained situations and remedies in plumbing or building terms or likened the health problem to certain household chores that get done every day.

Such things the patient and the family understands. A lexicon of big words and technical jargon to boot doesn't mean a thing, often causing more pain and apprehension.

Simply being in love can be complicated enough; being a senior can add to that complication. 1) "My ego and id...." 2) "The psychosomatic results...." 3) "Our psychodrama...." 4) "The societal foundation for our...." 5) "Our socioeconomic differences...." Save us!

1) "I have these feelings and impulses; my heart longs to embrace yours." You can make it simpler. "I'm in love with you; I want to hug and kiss you." 2) "I'm nervous and tongue-tied; just thinking about you sets me to tingling." 3) "We have a way to go, but we're working pretty well together and seem to be well suited." 4) "Whatever our differences, we have so much in common. We were meant to be together." 5) "What matters is our love. We will share what we have and work together for what we don't have. Your friends will be mine, mine yours."

You can do even better than that. Keep it simple.

I promised myself once, never would I use a word I

couldn't spell. Well, life is not quite that simple, and being a poor speller, I had to break the promise. But the intent of the promise has remained with me. Keep it simple.

As with many people, I exist in two linguistic worlds, One is the natural, simple world is which words usually mean what they say, and the other is a world in which simple thoughts are reduced to utter confusion by too large and pretentious words often of indefinite meaning because the speaker (or writer) using the bigger words doesn't really understand what he/she is saying.

Language has one purpose: to speak so as to be understood and to hear so as to understand. Ditto for reading and writing.

Even with the most complex of subjects, that purpose exists. Among scientists, for example, there may be a special vocabulary, but it is a common language within that group.

What good is saying something if no one can understand you? Most of us don't employ sixty thousand word vocabularies on a regular basis. In fact, most of us get by quite successfully with a few thousand words. Not that we couldn't add to our vocabularies, but the simple, straightforward words appeal to us. That does not mean we can't deal with complex ideas. We can and do. It's no accident that books by Carl Sagan and Stephen Hawking (i.e., on physics, cosmology, basic and unfathomed mysteries of the universe), Abraham Maslow and B.F. Skinner (psychology, cognitive skills), E.B. White (social commentaries, *Charlotte's Web* and *Stuart Little*), and many others are or were best sellers. Such authors put the most complex and involved ideas of universe and society and self into words we can understand. I would say our daily human relationships would benefit the most from the simplicity of our words.

Boston Light is one of the most famous lighthouses in the world, not because it guards historic Boston Harbor, not because it warns ships of the many treacherous islands which split the entrance to the harbor into two "roads," not because if you head east from the light you are bound for Portugal, not because the light is almost as old as America, but because the light flashes one, two, three. Since the earliest days of the lighthouse, one, two, three has been better known as the "I love you" lighthouse. One, two, three: I love you.

What could be simpler than that? Or more profound? Of all the dangers that abound, you are safe because I love you. We'll avoid the rocky shoals because I love you. One, two, three: woman and man's simplest words. Three words that light the world and guide your way. In Edna St. Vincent Millay's words, "And all the loveliest things there be / Come simply, so it seems to me."

Love is...

Love is the delicate smell of the earth
    after a summer rain.
Love is the scorching sun's blaze
    bursting through the clouds.
Love is as gentle as falling snow
    on a winter night.
Love is as tender as a mother's touch
    of her new newborn child
    and as raucous as a New Orleans
    jazz band at Mardi Gras.
Love is the ultimate faith
    that all is well with the world.
Love is the strength of mountains
    and the depth of the sea
    and stretches from horizon to horizon.
Love is believing in what is beyond the horizon.
Love is newness in an old world
    and faith in a new world built by two.
Love is one heart touching another
    in ways fresh and free of doubt.
Love is forsaking ego and self and making
    another's ego self shine.
Love is trust in tomorrow and the day
    after tomorrow.
Love is hope and dreams coming true.
Love is comforting arms in moments of trial,
    supporting arms in moments of endeavor,
    loving arms in moments of passion,
    uplifting arms in moments of need,
    welcoming arms forever.
Love is facing the fears of loving with courage.

Love is letting go of suspicion, mistrust.
Love is putting one's heart into another's hands,
      knowing it is safe from all harm.
Love is giving love without condition or restraint.
Love is life's meaning, the object of one's love
      life's purpose.
The return of love is one's joy.

In the Beginning...

In the beginning -
in the very beginning -
every idea
every creation
every act of love
is fresh and new -
in the beginning.

Every beginning
is hope - that out of darkness
will come a light,
that from nothing or
despair or chaos
will come newness -
clean, unspoiled, bright.

Reintroducing Adam and Eve

It's the briefest of stories, the creation of Adam, then Eve, and their transitory residency in the Garden of Eden.

In the Talmud's rendering of the myth, the ancient Assyrian female demon, Lilith, is present. (Remember the TV program "Cheers?" Frasier Crane's sour wife bore that name.) In Hebrew legend she is the symbol of sensual lust and often is considered Adam's first wife. (What, there was a second?)

In part that may account for the first woman's unenviable reputation as a seductress slut, lewd and slovenly, who, by the time the medieval church fathers got through with her, represented all women not to the manor born. (And the church fathers weren't so sure about those women, either.) It's not a coincidence that the doctrine of original sin was focused on sexual activity just at the time the church fathers were enforcing celibacy for priests, nor is it entirely coincidental that the church's reaction against the prevailing loose sexual mores of the noble/priestly classes became a call for a crusade to take back Jerusalem from the Islamic empire. War is great sublimation. It was all Eve's fault.

Adam's first wife? Second wife? Who knows. What is known from the Bible story is that Adam and Eve were one hundred and thirty years old when Eve birthed Seth, their third son, after which there is no further mention of Eve.

Adam lived another eight hundred years and begot more sons and daughters. To keep things in prospective, Cainan lived nine hundred and ten years and Jared eight hundred years and Methuselah nine hundred sixty nine years (the record), each long-lived "father" begetting and begetting -- all before Viagra. That may be miracle enough; if women lived as long, and kept birthing and birthing, there is the real miracle.

"In the beginning," *b'rayshith* in Hebrew, the earth and all living things were created, including adam, a Hebrew word meaning man or human being. After six days of creating, the Lord rested.

Refreshed, He thought, I'll make a woman, a helpmeet (often translated as wife, a sop to morality) for the adam. Adam (the name capitalized to signify first man), unlike all other creatures, was alone. In the paradise called Eden, he didn't recognize his singleness, yet when the Lord created woman, Adam gave the woman a name: Eve, in Hebrew, *chawwäd*; the name means "life."

If for no other reason than the names, one is drawn to the first pair. In a romantic view of the creation myth, Eve brought Adam to life. He was created and existed, a mere physical presence. With the coming of Eve, he achieved emotional life.

When the Greeks translated the Hebrew (and the Christian) literature, they used the word *genesis* for the "beginning" stories. Genesis means "coming into being." With Eve, Adam came into being.

The Adam and Eve stories are not a big deal in biblical literature; they serve the purpose 1) of tracing the genealogical (genetic) and religious lines of the Hebrew people directly to "the Creator" and 2) for Christians, the story provides the link between "Second Adam" (Jesus) and the original adam (the Lord's first adam, lower case). In Christian orthodoxy, Adam fell out of grace because of the fruit of a tree; Jesus potentially saved all adams (generic term) by being crucified on a pole or a cross made from a tree.

My interest in Adam and Eve is not theological, although theological implications are impossible to ignore. Writers of fiction and nonfiction have explored the allegory, the metaphors, the aptronyms, the onomastics of the Adam and Eve stories. I wish to play a bit with the myth, to draw from it what appear to be relevant if sometimes irreverent thoughts.

As with all great fictional characters, Adam and Eve mirror us. They are created (born) innocent. They learn the world and life contains both good and evil. They lose their innocence. They became hard working toilers of the land. They have children, one of whom is tragically delinquent. They are tested in a barren wilderness. Of all the genesis stories at the heart of the world's religions, Adam and Eve's story, as brief as it is, is the most revealing of our human nature.

In a patriarchal religion, woman, in this instance Eve, is not important. In the genesis stories, Eve is mentioned by name twice. The focus is on Adam's (man's) fall from God's grace. Eve serves as the instrument for that fall, nothing more, and she blames her devious role on a snake in the grass, an ancient phallic symbol.

The story's background is complicated; it is much more than an allegory deliberately misinterpreted or a metaphor badly twisted by theologians. The original intent is deeper. Early theologians must have believed that the "fact" of the Garden of Eden was too earthy for human beings, too sensual, too erotic to be fully explored.

The truth revealed in the story is this: At some point in her life, Eve gains knowledge about herself, knowledge being awareness, not facts. All the creatures had been created (she was the last) and had been instructed to multiply. Eve observed that each "came into season," their procreation time. She observed but did not understand; she saw but did not know what she was seeing; something was happening but she did not know what.

One day she experienced unfathomed feelings, strange

sensations, yearnings, a vague sense of incompleteness. She revealed her uneasiness to the snake, and sly creature that he was, he beguiled Eve into believing she'd understand herself once she ate a bit of fruit from the tree of knowledge. In effect, the snake talked Eve into doing what he didn't dare do.

You know what happened. Eve sensed her sexuality, her own procreative urges, her partnership need for Adam. Her vague awareness and her curious physical and emotional sensations come together in a sudden flash of knowing what she was: a sensuous, potential mother.

How tell Adam? He didn't understand. Eve's knowledge went over his head. Eve knew the truth of their being; they were, like all the other creatures, sexual beings. She had been awakened. How awake Adam?

Eve offered knowledge; Adam tasted the fruit; it was not enough. He saw only their nakedness. In one way, he was the first conservative. Don't upset the garden. He hid from knowledge. Seduced later, he delighted in it.

The Lord had warned the pair: "...of the tree of the knowledge of good and evil, thou shall not eat...for thee shall die." But it had been done. The need to know separated Adam and Eve from Eden forever.

Strange, but neither protested. The need of the human to seek knowledge seems to have been a fair trade for a finite life. Without knowledge, Adam and Eve were nothing. That's their appeal. They are we coming into being.

Those who would return to the mythical Eden strive in vain. And for what? Ignorance? An eternal, soulless life as God's gardeners? A life without thought? Sounds good sometimes, doesn't it. But a life without meaning? What good is that? A life without someone to love? Without purpose? Without emotion or feeling? What kind of life is that? It would be a lifeless existence and Eden would be a sterile garden, a beautiful, peaceful, trouble-free...prison.

> Eat
> Eve begged,
> and Adam ate,
> just a bite,
> and
> he saw
> their nakedness.
> Of all things,
> there,
> in bloom
> before his eyes,
> was his wife.
> She
> offered
> both an apple
> and herself.
> He
> "knew" her
> that day. To them,
> it was good.

The Lord had not foreseen their pleasure. He might have lived with His mistake were it not that their "knowing" was for other than procreation. That upset the Lord. It upset the authors of the faiths but not the storytellers. We all love a good story; especially we like a good love story.

And especially we like to speculate, fill in the missing lines, let our imaginations follow the many threads of potential stories. What if? What then? Who said and what did they say? The tiny story about humanity's genesis leads us to wonder and to suppose and to become storytellers ourselves, adding depth to one of the world's great myths.

* * *

Her name means "Life."

If there's a heroine in the Bible, it's Eve. It was her daring reach for knowledge that gave rise to the human race. That she is portrayed as the instrument of humanity's fall from grace is unfair, reflecting the male orientation of ancient Judaism, and later Christianity and Islam.

Originally, "original sin" (no pun intended) was the belief that all humans are predisposed to commit evil because Eve, then Adam, broke God's prohibition against eating the fruit that would give them knowledge of good and evil. Before Eve and Adam bit into the fruit, they did not know evil. Once they ate, it was supposed they not only knew badness, they would practice it. The original original sin was not sexual knowledge or activity. That would have been contrary to the Lord's command to multiply; it was knowing both right and wrong. And, of course, the theologians assumed all humans thereafter were more evil than good. (Otherwise why a "saving" or "restoring" religion?).

As suggested, the "original" sin of sex came thousands of years later, the Christian church's reaction to unrestrained sexual practices, gleefully, it seems, practiced by most of Christendom, the reverends condemning it (although both celibate and non-celibate clergy set themselves up as the experts in sexual matters), artists celebrating it with x-rated statuary and paintings (much of the eroticism blessed by the holy ones because it showed in living color what was not to be practiced), believers worried about going to hell but "doing it" anyway. And everyone blaming it on Eve.

Of course, Eve, with Adam, is a mythical figure, but in all the world's religious literature there is no more meaningful event than the mythical moment when humans gained the knowledge of good and evil. Her very name, "Life," is no accident. An unknown storyteller gave her--gave women-- the predominate role in the birth of the human race. That birth occurred when Eve sunk her teeth into the fruit from the tree of knowledge. The race has never been the same.

There's no evidence the fruit was an apple; there's no grounds for supposing a snake could talk; there's been no discovery of Eden's remains. We take the story as given, knowing it is fiction but enjoying it nonetheless, because somewhere, sometime, the human animal learned right from wrong, knew love and family, experienced hardship and turmoil and pressed on into the future, imperfect men and women creating imperfect civilizations.

From *b'rayshith*, humanity has tried to know God, genesis, the cosmos. We look for the big answers not realizing that most are the little answers within. We would be gods if we could. That's not what Eve sought; she sought the "why," the meaning of her life, and in her reach for that she is alleged to have separated humanity from God. Believe that if you must, but Eve did more: she gave every human being a measure of divinity, a heritage with one everlasting constant, the union of genders and the growth of love.

Credit our mythical Eve for that, for it is women who have created the family and on family is based civilization. Perhaps it was women who first sensed love. Who knows. Perhaps women are the true reflection of She who made us.

What Did They Say?

How we wish the storytellers
had told first words,
that under green umbrellas
of forest ferns
had been heard a hint of speech,
something, not racy
or juicy, some words that would reach
from then to now,
binding us to the beginning.
Was love spoken?
Was first touch animal knowing,
need, nothing more?
Say not that woman and adam
embraced in heat;
say their first knowing began
with tender words
we would speak now and listen to.
Say Adam held
Eve's hand, she his, each speaking, "Too,
do I love thee,"
words overdue since fruit's first bites.
We seek that phrase;
our lives "I love you" underwrites.
Naught approaches
the meaning of our fragile lives
more than three words.
Faint heart, sincere love word revives;
fault, love forgives;
hope, love affirms; dreams, love secures.
When A and E
first stood, kneeled, sat, amateurs

(misuse of word?),
unsure, shy, innocent, in doubt,
they must have talked,
used words we should speak, the devout
love expressions
we need to use and hear. What were they?
What did Eve say
that won Adam? And Adam say?
We seek those sounds
now, to say to the one we love
and from that one
to hear sweet music from above,
birthed in Eden.

46

All Lovers Would
(from a longer, unpublished poem)

       ...All lovers would
share Adam and Eve's first hushed touch
of hand to hand, and if they could,
share the gentle, caressing strokes
of their caring, their hankering,
share in their discoveries, one
and the other awakening.

All lovers rejoice in Adam
and Eve. Their sexuality
was new and fresh. Every moment
discovery; the duality
that led them to a harmony
of spirit and flesh was the first
human experience of love
from which our humanity burst.

Everyone who loves another
would taste each sweet kiss as the first,
feel each caress as something new,
hear each loving word with a thirst.
Every lover would be first Eve,
first Adam, and each "knowing" would
be as wonderful as the first,
new shared depths explored - if we could.

All lovers are jealous of Eve
and Adam. They were the first pair
of lovers to know ecstasy,

the first pair of lovers to share
in the pleasure of the other,
the first to know the excitement
of flesh pressed to flesh in delight
of a union magnificent.

Once

Once,
Eve,
mother of all women,
reached
out
for Adam, maybe more
than
once.
She reached out for him once
and
that
made all the difference.

Illusion?

Would that we could hold a hand on Eve's
or Adam's heart, feel the quickened pulse therein,
know that from the first
the heart did beat in wonder.
It's in the mind, scoffers say,
but we know better.
The mind tells us what fools we be;
the heart reveals that even fools
would give their all
to lovers be.

Love is Spiritual

It's not commonly expressed today, but love has a spiritual facet that shines beyond the "let's get it on" mentality, the openly and seeming exclusive equation of love with sex.

The original word "spirit" separated itself from the physical, as in body and soul, the physical body distinct from the mind.

I've pointed out numerous times that lovemaking, the physical uniting of two people, is an important aspect of romantic love and that passion and the sharing of passion can and should be frequent and wonderful events. All things considered, amour must be expressed physically, and rightfully so.

What I'm presenting here for your thought is that love also exists on another level, a spiritual level which ultimately or basically is more important than the physical.

"He is adorable." "She is my inspiration." "Our love is awesome." Such adjectives are (were) spiritual or religious words.

In applying them to love and love relationships, I'm not looking for a theological argument, simply pointing out that love has its religious and/or spiritual overtones. The one you love is elevated above mere mortals. That is as it should be: your loved one is special, unique, the one among many.

I caution you: do not say your loved one is "awful." That word means awe-inspiring, but in today's careless usage it means just the opposite. "Awesome" might be a better choice.

However you want to praise your loved one, he/she

deserves the high place in which you place her/him. As the Psalmist said, "This is my beloved...."

And your beloved says, "Believe in me," and you do. You believe he or she loves you, loves (in the sense we're talking about here) only you, will care for you, support you (emotionally, that is), will sacrifice for you. Your beloved has become a lesser god or goddess in your eyes. To the rest of the world he may be a clod or she may be a mouse, but to you he is Apollo; she a lioness.

Believing in your partner, you are rewarded. Life is not a bleak trek toward nowhere; it's an adventure of the soul. You are not alone; you are in the arms of sustaining love. You are not an insignificant, almost non-person, individual; you are somebody vitally and eternally important. You are not a failure; you are potential and promise. You are not weak; you are made strong.

That relationship is awesome. You adore your partner because he/she helps make you better than you believed you might be. It is she or he who inspires you to fulfill your potential. Your partner is life and light and beauty and fills your existence with all that is true and holy. Being loved bestows those blessings upon you.

Then, and only then, when you return your beloved's gifts in like kind, are you able to prove your love for him/her.

Is it heresy to equate the love of a man or a woman with the love of a deity? I don't think so, not if that person is your world and your universe. He or she cannot create a universe or a planet or an ocean or even a flower, but in a sense, the one who loves you does create the world in which you live.

And in turn, you create his or her new world.

I say "new" because until we love and find love, our world is incomplete and of lesser worth. When love and a faithful lover comes to us, it's as a new day aborning and a new life birthed.

Emerson said, "I believe I shall some time cease to be an individual, that the tendency of the soul is to become Universal...." Am I misusing the great American philosopher when I suggest that in love one does cease to be an individual and becomes a pair? Emerson never would suggest that the individual ceases to be; he would insist that the individual is greater when part of a larger whole. He wasn't speaking about the love of two people, but the truth applies. And in this there is the truth that the soul tends toward the universal impulse called love.

Later I write about reality and dreams (images). The image of love is within each lover; the reality of that love is greater than either lover. Emerson would agree, for that greater reality is the universal theme of love.

Like all spiritual quests, this test: not to avoid or retreat from love but to risk whatever will be by running forward toward newness with love in your heart.

That's what I mean by spiritual. Love is a reason to be and to have faith in our being. Amen.

A Poem for Emily Dickinson

From the beginning, the Logos:
all things ascend from the Word.
She said we are nothing without
the Word that made us and keeps us.

Storytellers, singers, poets
found the Word, told and retold it
by the campfires and in the caves,
mystery Word, holy Word, divine.

When the earth trembled, she told it,
when fear howled about, she spoke it;
from within her dark inferno
the Word singer wrote down the Word,
illuminated her own doubts
and turned back the vile self-darkness.
Frightened, tortured, her clear meter
said, Hear, you are the Word made flesh.

And the Word was Joy; and the Word
was Awe; and the word was Love, and
the Word singer overcame dark
doubt with the Word: Awe, Joy, Love.

And the Word was made into flesh.
All the singers who sang her Word,
those who listened and joined in song,
they became the Word: ECSTASY.

I Believed in You

As I walked with you,
my hand in your hand,
you spoke. What you said
entered me, became
my thought as later
the smell, taste, color,
size, and shape of you
entered eager heart.
I was part of you;
I was your laughter,
your tears, your trials,
your victories, and
your hopes and dreams.
Your sweet breath fed me;
your heart engulfed me;
your touch strengthened me.
"We" became greater
than "I," you more than
myself. With such thoughts
love was spiritual.
I believed in you,
prayed you believed in me.

About Seasons

Beyond doubt,
      Summer is best.
Summer is our
      Passion, desire,
Grand illusions
      Becoming truth,
Hot, musky, the
      Body covered
In delicious
      Sensual sweat.
Because of that
      I like Spring too:
Forecast, promise,
      Erotic dreams
Which, if this life
      Is truly just,
Will come true (Soon
      Enough?) in Summer.
Fall can be nice
      If our Summer
Was what Spring had
      Promised us,
Otherwise Fall
      is but blunt hint
Of more ice, slush,
      Of bleak Winter,
Frigid season,
      But not because
The sun is low,
      Simply because
What Spring promised
      Never was, 'though
Trust that holy
      Promise we do.

What Happens After the Perfect Love?

It never was any of my doing, just a series of sociological coincidences, the sociological awareness coming much later in life. For a time I was raised among a mix of old Yankee and Portuguese fisherman families and then for most of my teen years in the city among mostly Irish and Italian families. From my earliest years I remember a few people who were or who had been in the entertainment business: playwriters, musicians, a Hollywood camera man. When we moved to the city I came in contact with a number of former vaudevillian people. And when in college, serving a small congregation, among the parishioners were several carnival people, the small town their winter home. And later I served a suburban congregation in which there were many former vaudevillians and early radio people.

I bring this up because of one former song and dance man of Italian origin. One day he began a conversation by naming the people in the community and specifically our church who had been on the stage. He ended his recitation with the suggestion that vaudeville could be revived, if only to allow the many people he named to relive their acts and show off what once they had done. For several years the resulting show was a major hit.

That man always ended our conversation with "L'alba di ogni giorno ti il mio saluto," may the dawn of every day bring you my greeting.

I asked him once where the phrase originated. Somewhat sheepishly he confessed that it was an old Sicilian saying most often found on tombstones. "Even though it's supposed to be a message from the dead," he said, "I like it. Every new day I would like to greet everyone. It's kind of

56

like a love poem."

Indeed it was.

I thought of that man and his touching sentiment as the woman who sat before me spoke.

She told me she had had the perfect husband, the perfect lover, the perfect mate; even several years after his death, her image of their perfect marriage had not diminished in her memory. She used the word "perfect" many times.

"But why are you here?"

"I don't know. I really don't know."

Unconsciously, I think, she wanted me to guess, not as a game but that perhaps I could come up with something to explain her unhappiness. She was at mid age, and, I silently guessed, because she had come to a clergyman, she might be going through a kind of long delayed bereavement, reinforced and complicated, maybe, by menopause.

Thankfully, I didn't voice either thought. Instead, I asked her to tell me about her husband. That seemed a safe place to start. I did not know her or her husband. She had called and had asked for an appointment.

That first day, as she talked about her perfect husband, I kept waiting for a shoe to drop: he was perfect, she wasn't; he was perfect except...; he died, she didn't, and she felt guilty. None of that. Their romance was perfect, according to her, and remained perfect for the dozen years of their marriage. If she carried a dark secret, it was well hidden. I came to believe there was no imperfection, at most minor annoyances, none of which had threatened the marriage.

Nor was there a sense of a long season of bereavement. He had had cancer, his death was inevitable, they had dealt with the fact for two years, and when he died, it was natural and expected. His death saddened her, but she had come to grips with it and with her loss.

Yet the woman was deeply troubled. Over a period

of time, I began to sense what Emerson meant by dragging around the "corpse of your memory."

At one meeting I suggested that her memory of her perfect husband was what she had let it become: a dead weight anchor rather than a wellspring. Memories, I told her, can be a foundation upon which to build a future or they can be a petrified past for which there is no future.

She took offense at the suggestion. "Our love was perfect; you diminish it."

"On the contrary," I said. "Stay in the past or risk the future."

Now she was angry, but she did ask what I meant.

"If a memory cannot hold its own with new memories-in-the-making," I told her, "perhaps the old memory needs to be rethought, its proper place found, not allowed to be so all-consuming that no other memories, old or new, have their place."

"That's...." I didn't let her finish.

"You found and for a time had your supreme love and lover. He died, and for you, love died with him. That's a normal feeling, but part of the premise is false. Your loved one and your mutual love affair ended with his death. You are left with memories--but love did not die."

"No."

"No what?"

"No, love did not die. What does that mean for me?"

"Perhaps you won't find another someone to love, but to shut love out of your life is no way to treat a memory of love."

"I've done that, haven't I." It was a statement, not a question.

I didn't respond directly. "What you've done is let your love memory become an unhealthy obsession."

When that woman's perfect love affair ended, she believed no other love affair could match it. Perhaps she was correct.

But what came through, what she couldn't figure out, was that she had the need to give love to someone and the need to be loved by someone. By denying the possibility of ever loving again, she recognized neither present need.

Even when she did recognize and admit her needs, she could not face the possibility of taking the next steps. "I don't dare," she explained, "What if it's not perfect?" She meant a new love and a new lover.

Already she had made a major concession. As perfect as her former love was, she was allowing the potential for a new love to enter her thoughts.

"Imperfection is a risk, isn't it?"

I remember a long silence followed by a question. "What else?"

I thought we might just let the achievement sink in, pick it up later, but her entire body language demanded my reply. "Not daring the risk doubles the sorrow. You lost your perfect husband, and you deny yourself a second chance at love. In a metaphorical sense, two lovers died. You, the second one, by choice. Oh, the body lives, the mind functions, but the heart is stilled--and that's sad." It was an insensitive response.

It took her a long time to react, and when she did, it was simply, "I've been sad too long."

It took a while. She had to come to an agreement with herself that the potential for a new, loving relationship was not a betrayal of her husband. She did that one day with a statement: "I don't think S... wanted me to die with him."

I was sure of that, otherwise he wouldn't have been perfect and his love would have been selfish. I voiced only the "sure" part of the thought.

I don't know if the woman ever found someone. It sounds cold, even cruel, to say she stopped dragging around the corpse of her dead husband, but she did, cherishing the memories but not allowing her life to end in the past.

I wonder sometimes whether I did her a good or a harm. She freed herself from an emotional burden. That was good. She acknowledged she might risk love again if.... That was good. It's the "if" that disturbs me after all these years because "if" is so risky.

I comfort myself by saying every relationship has its risks, and every free individual must deal with the consequences in his or her own way. And there is another way of considering the pain and grief resulting from a lost love. Had there been no love, there would be no grief and no pain for its loss. The question then becomes a question about risking loving. Is the reality of love greater than not loving at all?

What disturbs me more are those who won't or can't give love a second chance. Often that seems contrary to our human nature, denial for the sake of denial. Locking the heart away in a closet of dusty memories is not, to me, natural or healthy.

Yes, there are risks, but a risk not taken seems, to me again, a denial of life. Not only that, I know too many second marriages, "in partnerships," the current buzz phrase, unions, whatever word fits, that outshine and surpass the first.

* * *

Only in the past few years has the word "closure" been associated with death and/or great loss. Language is forever changing and evolving; perhaps the twenty-first century will add a whole meaning to "close" and "closure."

No dictionary of which I know presently includes within the twenty-five or thirty definitions of close and closure anything of comfort.

I know the intent, however, and it is both honorable and necessary: to come to terms with death or loss. Unfortunately, the word closure seems to treat death as the end of an event, when in fact the event, the long, loving relationship of two people, was so much more.

Nothing in the word closure implies moving on or dealing with cherished memories while reaching toward yet unfulfilled hopes.

A life, in the instance of death, has ended, but is that the end of it? There are memories of experiences, learning, sharing, trials, and love that are not ended. One shouldn't close them out. The hope is that upon such memories life can be rebuilt. A chapter in one's life has ended, not one's life.

Losing a love by death, divorce or other separation is sad and soul wrecking. Journeying headlong into the future with your partner, the sudden deceleration, the resulting emotional injury, leaves you a wreck. Never will you completely close the book on that part of your life, and never should you.

We are of the present in chronological time, but we are what the past has contributed to us. We cannot undo or deny the past, even if we want to, and we should not live entirely in the past even if we wish to.

Not to become overly philosophical, but the present is a fleeting moment. It is now but at the same moment it is becoming the past. Watching an hourglass is the perfect analogy. Above, a grain of sand is now. It flows through a tiny hole and immediately becomes time gone by and piles up below with all the other grains of sand that have passed.

Look at the hourglass. Above, grains of sand that have not yet flowed into the past is the future. We are not just a momentary present and a past; if the analogy contains truth, we also are future. The hourglass is the whole of us: past, present, future. No hourglass works unless there is future.

I don't remember using the analogy with the woman cited above, but that's what she was missing, a sense of the future. Fixated on the past, she saw no future, and even when she acknowledged the need to draw upon the past to give a future the potential for being, she hesitated because of the risk that the future could not equal the glories of the past.

For some, the opposite might be true, that the bad, evil, unfulfilling past will be duplicated in the future. That's also a risk; then future happiness is denied because one doesn't dare to partake of the unknown future; eat, drink and be merry because tomorrow we die, pleasures instead of happiness because one cannot trust her/himself in the future-- and trusts nobody.

Life is in the future. All our hopes and dreams and happiness lie somewhere in the future. Fearful, we know also that the future can be rich and wondrous. The good life is yet to be.

Death Watch

How quietly death passes by the men.
One is taken with barely a nod,
his absence noted but not for long,
his name seldom will be spoken again.
Someday someone will think to ask,
"Where's Earl? Where's he gone?" And when told,
"Oh, we all go sometime,"
and he'll step into line.

Not so the women. They take death personally.
When a man passes, it's their man
whether it is or not. Death is a scam,
life's dirty trick played on women
and must be exposed for what it is
and fought if only with proper mourning
and forgiveness one last time
for "the next man might be mine."

About Them
(Lines from a longer, unpublished memorial poem)

The door opened reluctantly,
welcoming the one,
then hurriedly closed,
leaving the other on the portico
lost and alone.

-       -   -   -

...when they stood together before the door,
they knew its meaning.
Its presence was in their birth.
They needed no knock.
The door would open in its own time;
they were prepared for that.
They were not prepared for their separation,
the one into eternal dream free night,
the other into remembering.

Voyage Among the Stars

Should I in a subsequent life
voyage among the stars,
by heaven's light I'd search for you,
most precious pilot star.
And when I've found your brilliant light,
I'll climb its shining beam;
I'll hold you close and wrap us both
within a moonbeam's dream.
Burning with celestial fire,
you've set my heart ablaze;
I'm caught in your star-burning heat,
your sparks like love bouquets.
Another life I dare not wait;
you've drawn me to your flame.
My morning star and evening star
in earth's time you became.
Should I voyage among the stars,
my single thought would be
where is she, how find her and love
her through eternity?
Once, lost and lonely shooting stars,
our helix paths were crossed;
not fading into endless space,
our joined lives we embossed,
rekindled the fires of our lives,
and in love refound hope
in sunbeam sparks and moon glow dreams,
love's grand kaleidoscope
of sweet scents and rainbow colors
and whispered earthy sound.
Should I all heaven search, nothing
will outshine what I've found.

Love Words

Words are tricky little things, and they can get us into plenty of trouble, especially the written word, if we aren't careful.

When a word is spoken, its subtle meaning is transmitted by verbal inflections and by the speaker's body language. Even then there's plenty of room for misinterpretation and misunderstanding, as any would-be lover can prove.

The written word has no such helper. It may have modifiers, adjectives and adverbs, employed on its behalf, but ultimately a word has to stand on its own. Thus when read, a word may not mean what the writer intends but what the reader perceives. Many a disagreement begins with, "You said...." Ever been there?

I used to tell my students whether they realized it or not, they spoke at least three "English" languages. There was the language they spoke in the classroom (well, most of the time); there was the language they used with their mother (simple and pure); there was the language they used in the streets (and growing more crude all the time). I hoped they wouldn't confuse the three.

Additionally, for some students, there was a different manner of speaking. Foreign-born students frequently had the remnants of their country of origin tongue, and in families that cherished their heritage, a few students were truly bilingual.

The first lesson of misused language came to me early in my life. On rare occasions, my mother would fix a very special lemon pudding for my brother's and my dessert. She always served it from an antique cut glass bowl.

One day as my mother was bringing the treat to the

table, she and I shared a joke of some kind, and my brother felt left out and said something to announce his displeasure. My mother reprimanded him, to which he replied, "You're always...with Bob."

I was nine, I think, so my brother was six. Anyway, plop went the cut glass dish on my brother's head, the wonder pudding streaking his face and shoulders. He had no idea what he had said. I knew the words but I didn't know what they meant. Apparently my mother knew the words, and she must have known what they meant.

Should I laugh or cry? My all-time favorite dessert was all over my brother. I could have cried just for that. If ever the guilty was innocent, it was my brother. He had used a forbidden word and had been punished--and he didn't know why. Trying to hide my laughter, my belly ached. My brother and I still talk about it. It was the only time my mother ever raised a hand to either of us. My brother remembers that; I remember the word lesson, too.

Which is not to say my language was purified; it is to say I knew which language to use where--most of the time. Even now I slip occasionally and can but hope that amid my faults others will find greater virtues and praise them.

That lesson was reinforced just last week (as I write this). A neighbor, very religious in her practice and very conservative in her theology, asked me if I had ever used a certain word in my preaching. The word she used has long been a gutter word, although one of its origins is the corruption of a man's name. I told her that much. Later I traced the word to the early Low Dutch; I have not told her of that other origin. I don't believe the conversation would be very well received. Actually, whatever the origin, I couldn't believe a preacher would use the word. It has had but one meaning for well over a hundred years. His use must have been a very, very careless slip of the tongue.

Of course, it might have been the right word in a different setting, but a sound preacher would have found a suitable (for a church worship service) synonym.

The corruption of our speech is happening at a rapid rate, thanks, I think, largely to television. My school children (sorry, young people) used to sing popular songs that when I was their age would have been frowned upon even by my social peers, and we lived in urban tenement houses among the bluest of blue collar workers and before that among poorly educated coastal fishermen.

But we've taken a wide detour, the excuse being to impress upon you the care with which one must speak and/ or write words of love. You can disagree, but I believe you show respect for the one you love by using the best words you know when telling her/him so. And I believe you honor him or her by eliminating improper words. It just seems the thing to do, if for no other reason than to elevate your good thoughts to their highest level.

That said, the wonder and the mystery of the English language can, because many words have multiple meanings, cause difficulty, one meaning to the speaker, another meaning to the hearer. Or one chooses the wrong synonym, or one makes mistakes because of improper homonyms.

When the relationship is such that the hearer can ask "What do you mean?" without getting angry, there is hope. Often when we attempt love and loving words, we get tongue-tied. In the early stages of a budding romance, nervous and filled with doubt, words come out wrong. Speaking, sometimes we can correct our mistakes, but if we write our thoughts down on paper, the words stand as written.

There is a simple vocabulary of love words: we, our, beauty, faith, trust, dreams, share, care, support, with (as in with you), together, future, forgive, understand--the list goes on and on, simple words that reinforce the one big word: love.

Such words cannot be spoken too often nor can they be heard too often. They are the verbal foundation upon which a loving partnership is built and sustained. They must be spoken every day; they have no substitutes, nor is there a substitute for speaking them.

Choose your words carefully; use simple words. The listener or reader will give the simple words the enormous meaning you intend, and of your love there will be no misunderstanding.

You will have other faults and will need forgiveness for them, but you will never be faulted for expressing love in your most eloquent and natural voice. "Do I love you? Let me tell you how much. I...."

In *The Arabian Nights*, (often better known by its subtitle, "A Thousand and One Nights"), a caliph, a prince of Baghdad, took a new woman to his bed each night, and after enjoying her physically, he asked her for a story. Apparently the stories (at least that's the idea behind the book) were not very good because the caliph had each woman beheaded the next morning.

Then along came Scheherazade. She kept her head by telling a thousand and one stories the caliph liked. The caliph has gone, not remembered by name; Scheherazade has lasted through the centuries. Telling your love story to the one you love is much like that. Each night (and day) you have the opportunity and the obligation to tell a story, as it were. Do it poorly, off with your head (not literally, of course); do it well and life will be long and lovely.

Each story begins with some form of "I love you" and is followed by the inclusive pronouns "we" or "our." It's that simple--and that profound.

The First Great Gift

(from a longer, unpublished poem)

When speech was free to impart
depths of feelings, how did our tongues
give words to love and romance
that later poets would write?
When did language first unite
words of love with tender embrace,
word-paint acts with human grace?
From the grunter to Solomon's
Songs, from squawker to Shakespeare's
sonnets: how long? What mother tongue
uttered first the phrase among
all word bytes, I love you and need you,
and had it heard as love's due?
When from wordless, gruff beast sounds
to tender voices singing love?

Always the words; we needed the words.
First the touch and then the words;
words made the touch soft and tender,
sweet, rich voice gender to gender;
language of the heart; language of
the hearth, language of the home,
mating words, family words, caring
words, sharing words, man saying
loving words, woman saying
loving words. The beginning.

Criticism

Criticism should float down like feathers
from the soft underbelly where down grows
and touch the intended kindly,
tenderly,
unlike the bellicose prose
that cuts to hurt because it comes
from tooth and fang whose only cruel purpose
injury.
Speak with care, softly,
the words that one day may separate us.

"Our," A Love Word

Without debate,
the most precious
words he could say
are "I love you."
Above all words,
those are most dear.
And yet there is
one other word
that means as much:
"Our." Not yours, mine
but what we have
together, as in
our plans, our hopes,
our endeavors,
our future. Then
I know he means
the "I love you."

Lexicon

What can I say that's fresh and new?
What words will delight you,
stir your passion, light your fire,
regard me with loving desire?

I know, Fowler's English Usage;
of love words surely no shortage.
Love dismissed. See "Stock Pathos."
Fowler gave me the double-cross.
Love: see also "Hackneyed Phrases."
His omission amazes.
Love is pathos and hackneyed?
Come on, Fowler, love words I need.

I turned to Oxford's Companion
to English Language. There's none,
not one word of love nor hint
that love exists, no well phrased glint
even of words I might purloin
and use, plunder as my coin.
Not counterfeit would they be,
simply borrowed and said by me.

There's no help; I'm left on my own.
Original seeds not sown,
I pick the hackneyed phrases
and hope that speech alone blazes
like the radiant sun this day,
that when I've said, she will say,
"Your words are beauty and true;
my words are plain, I do love you."

So What is a Love Poem?

Love is...? That's a good question, isn't it. When we're in love, we know it or think we do, but define it? That's hard because love is not brainy; it's visceral, feeling, not intellectual, given to oohs and ahs but not to verbal explanations. Love is wonder and awe, hopes and dreams, sunrise and sunset, beauty and light—and we don't do very well verbalizing our perceptions and responses to those feelings either.

To misuse a line T.S. Eliot stole from Lancelot Andrewes, "The word within a word, unable to speak a word," Andrewes's "Verbum infans, the Word without a word," illustrates the lover's and the poet's problem. That's because love is an abstraction. It can't be measured; it's real but it's not concrete; it's presence or its absence is felt but not seen.

Eliot was speaking of the earthly manifestation of his god in the figure of Christ. I intend no such theological statement, only that "The word within a word" and "the Word without a word" harbors great truth: the thought exists before the word is spoken, the thought is more profound than the word, words are inadequate to the thought.

The poet Marianne Moore got it right, I think, when she said we must create "imaginary gardens with real toads in them" and echoed Eliot's "words within a word" with "The power of the visible / is the invisible."

Love is a word, sometimes misused, often overused, but when it is a genuine word expression, the simple word means so much that is not said. When love is spoken from the heart, it contains a universe of invisible, unseen emotions, including the flowered, heavenly garden image of one's dreams. All so esoteric, shared with one only. A love garden (dream)? That's what Moore means by "real toads."

Reality. And the love reality is kissing a toad and having it turn into a prince or a princess. Or being a toad and being kissed by the one who loves you and who turns you into.... you know, a prince or a princess!

When we're in love we know it, but try describing that love to someone else. It's nearly impossible; really, it is impossible. You can describe the affects love has upon you; that's about all you can do. And when love fails? We're not any better off. We can voice our pain and utter a different kind of oh and groan our misery and endure the darkness, but we're not defining love.

That's the nature of love. When it's present, rejoicing; when it's absent or withdrawn, agony. If I could decree it so, we would know only the rejoicing. Lost love, failed love, unrequited love would be banished.

But that's not to be, and upon second thought, perhaps the failed or not responded to or lost love serves a purpose. To lose a love or to fail at love or to offer love without reciprocation makes us know all the more the value of love, and if there's a second opportunity to love, we know how much more we have to put into it and how much harder we have to work to realize love's potential.

Recently I watched and listened as a young girl auditioned for a part in a musical. She was thirteen. To show off her talents, she chose to sing a medley of very moving love songs. She did okay and people liked her voice. So did I, but I was uncomfortable; she sang about things she neither knew nor appreciated nor had experienced; she was like the mockingbird, a beautiful voice singing someone else's songs. Singing without the fact of experience, her songs lacked the essential elements of genuine feeling. She had not been there, done that. Her singing lacked truth.

Had she ever truly been in love? Had she had her heart broken? Had she lost the light and love of her life?

Did she have any understanding of the words she sang from "Madam Butterfly" and "Porgy and Bess?"

She still was a child, struggling with all the complications that are present when a girl-child seeks to become a woman. She, or more likely her advisors, tried to fool the listeners into believing she was what she wasn't. She didn't get the part. I think, had she sung from "Annie" or "You're a Good Man, Charlie Brown," or songs by characters more her age and experience, the children's songs from "The Sound of Music," for instance, she might have succeeded.

In a life that's full of opposites, it's hard to know up if you don't know down, sense light if you've never experienced darkness, feel love if you've never lost it, or pain over its loss if you've never had it. For a thirteen year old to try to convey a depth of feeling about love and lost love is just not believable. Young people should be young people, not try to be what they aren't, which is one reason I react so negatively to children made up by their parents to impersonate movie stars and models.

Experience. Having it may be tough, learning from it even tougher, benefiting from it toughest of all. So we ask, what is love? And what makes a poem a love poem? I have to retreat to I don't know, by which I mean what I've said previously: love or its absence is feeling and is not given readily to intellectual analysis.

You may wonder about the inclusion of certain poems, how in the world I can call them love poems. I'm not going to defend a single one, simply revert to "Because I say so."

My hope is not that you find yourself reflected in any one or several poems but that in some instances I say what you might like to say or express what you might express-- or at least touch your circumstance with understanding and sympathy, if not empathy, and/or proclaim your joy and sense of happiness.

Reading poetry takes a bit of practice, unlike reading prose where the temptation is to skip words here and there while maintaining the overall flow. Children appreciate poetry because they respond immediately to the rhythm, and when the rhythm is like a heart beat, they know intuitively the elemental feeling the poet is attempting to convey.

Adults, so sophisticated, want to ignore the essential poetic rhythms because it's man and woman against the natural flow of nature. Subdue rather than join the flow; smite rather than become part of the beat; deny the very nature of human nature, all business-like and stern.

Nobody remembers his name or his poetry; he was one of the romantic age poets who wrote little and was read even less. He once asked,

> If there were dreams to sell
> What would you buy?
> Some cost a passing bell,
> Some a light sigh....
> If there were dreams to sell,
> Merry and sad to tell,
> And the crier rang the bell,
> What would you buy?

The author's name is Thomas Beddoes, and in his way he got the whole of life right. Dreams and the wake up part are both merry and sad; you can't buy one without the other, from Charles Lamb's "I loved a Love once, fairest among women / Closed are her doors on me...." to Hartley Coleridge's "...behold / the love-light in her eye; / her very frowns are fairer far / than smiles of other maidens are!" to Elizabeth Barrett Browning's "The face of all the world is changed, I think, / Since first I heard the footsteps of thy soul...." to Tennyson's "Tears from the depth of some divine despair / Rise in the heart, and gather in the eyes... / Deep as first love, and wild with all regret, - / O Death in Life, the days that are no more."

With love in one's heart, one might wish to return to the so-called romantic age. But romance is ageless; the romantic age of the nineteenth century stands out only because so many wonderful and creative men and women burst forth at the same time with unequaled romantic expressions, in art, in music, in words and songs. Perhaps it is true: never before or since have so many, collectively, written with such feeling about the merry and the sad love of their lives.

I mention one more poet from the romantic age, Arthur William Edgar O'Shaughnessy, who died young (age thirty-seven) and whose few poems I have found are either bitterly humorous and/or reflectively profound. From the latter, "...For each age is a dream that is dying, / Or one that is coming to birth."

How well seniors know that. However the loss of a former loved one, that age is dying. With a new late-in-life loved one, a new age is being born. Yet, in one's senior years, love is not always long lasting; the possibility for the death of love is ever present; senior dreams do die.

The dreamer doesn't die, only the dreamer's dream. The dreamer may be old; the dreams are young women's and young men's dreams, and with such dreams, the old are forever young.

When love fails, there is the temptation to write bitter words; love is lost, then remorse, then rancor comes and turns love into hate. To feel that is natural; life has betrayed us. To let hate replace love seems to be a denial of the love one once had for someone, the good, while it lasted, tarnished. I go back to O'Shaughnessy as a way of dealing with that. He had lost a love and had "made another garden... / For my new Love...." In his imagery, his old love returned and walked through his new garden. "She made the white rose-petals fall, / And turn'd the red rose white." Yes, there is bitterness in those lines, but the way O'Shaughnessy handles them, there is humor, too. She "laid the garden waste," but he "left the dead rose where it lay / And set the new above." The dream had died, not the dreamer.

A Thousand Words; Ten Thousand Dreams

Each night I whispered
a thousand words to you,
and each night I dreamed
ten thousand dreams, too.

Unheard, unknown by you,
these thoughts I whispered near.
My inmost soul-born words
spoke my heart's truth clear:

There beside me, you dreamed
our dreams, your heart beating
in rhythm with my own,
bespeaking love's greeting.

Each night I whispered that.
Each night I reaffirmed
my pledge, silent love thoughts
your silent trust confirmed.

What Means a Dream?

My night image so real:

Before us a cottage wreathed
in ten thousand blossoms,
the doorway arched with
red and white and pink roses.
We approach, your left hand
in my left hand, my right
guiding you under the arch
and toward the door.

What's inside the villa
or what happens there
is not revealed.
When next I see,
we stand in another doorway,
hand in hand, before us a field of flowers
and birds and butterflies, endless;
no horizon lies in distance.

We entered under roses;
we exit, awed by beauty.
We do not move, take no step.
We just stand, breathless,
squeezing hands. Then I awake,
thrilled to shaking
and shivering with fear.

What does the dream mean?

Say, Daisy Petal

Petals cast to the winsome wind,
"She loves me; she loves me not."
I catch the daisy hope blown back,
the twirling sign of love I sought.
She loves me! Yet, in the rapture-
moment of falling flower proof,
no petal speaks endearing words,
signing only, nodding, aloof,
the measure of love left unsaid.
She loves me! But one loves kitty
and pony, a movie, a book,
all things cute or warm or pretty.

The petals do not say if love
is more than that, if the love part
is ardor and passion also,
if the loved one has lost her heart
to me. One can love a puppy,
one is not in love with the same.
So, mute petal, she does love me,
but do I set her heart aflame?

Mayspark

In the dark of September nights,
scratching ashes of a long ago fire,
twisted fingers seek a Mayspark,
the once bright flame that, though brief its light,
keeps one heart lit in afterglow.
Cold ashes lie still, untouched by time,
and silent, tell of lost passion.
To external touch, the fire is dead,
and those who lived and loved and pledged
before its light and warmth gone, unknown.
Such fires were secret built by two,
and when cold, only two remember.
Or one remembers, wondering
if in this September of their lives
the other remembers, too, and,
unseen on the ashes' farther side,
is bent in search of the Mayspark.

Lovemaking Face to Face

When, forty years ago, the long debated issue of "sex" education in the public school came to a head in the community in which I was working, and it seemed likely the school committee would finally recognize the necessity of offering such a program, I suggested to two violently opposed clergymen that they take a vacation. At least, I suggested, be out of town the night the school committee was to vote its decision.

I don't know where the two men went, only that they did not appear before the committee to voice their personal and institutional opposition. There were plenty of others willing to do that, but they did not carry the day. Courses were introduced and in time were accepted and appreciated for what they were: greatly needed education in the cultural, psychological, social, and physical facts of human sexuality.

Humans are sexual beings; in fact, most life is. The lowest forms of life multiply by cell division, but flowers and fruits, insects, animals of all kinds, and that includes the human animal, reproduce because of the male/female nature of the various species. It is not only fact, it is natural.

One of the arguments against sex education (that phrase is a misnomer) was that sex was not a fit topic of conversation among genteel people. That's a lie, of course. Princes and paupers have been talking about sex since history was first recorded. And before language and alphabets, ancient artists were drawing all those "dirty pictures" on cave walls in India, China and France.

The reason I say "sex education" is a misnomer is one of the reasons I vigorously supported the program and course material. Of course the human reproductive process is discussed. As the grade levels increase so does the amount and detail of that process. Facts of life are essential; an informed young person is an intelligent person.

But there is a great deal more being offered in our public schools, and rightfully so, not the least being the concepts of love, including amour, and the meaning of and responsibilities of loving someone. I always found it ironic that some clergymen who required premarital counseling objected to a school curriculum that reached young people when they first needed information and guidance.

A sound curriculum goes far beyond providing sexual information. It deals with the entire range of partnership, something many of us learned the hard way--to our disadvantage.

By mandate, history is the common core of public school curriculums. You remember your history courses: Indian wars, revolution, wars with Spain and France and England, war with Mexico, two world wars, Korea, Asian wars.

History tells us little about the people. We know the funny clothes worn by the Pilgrims, but what do we know about the fifteen thousand years of Indian life and love, children born of love, families, or even Pilgrim family life?

Do we suppose we invented love? Or that men, mostly, and women spent their entire lives at war? History doesn't tell us about men and women; we have to go to a poet, Walt Whitman, two hundred and fifty years after the Pilgram landing to hear about the love of people, and manly and womanly love.

There's a blackout, deliberate and ongoing, because someone thought Adam and Eve were the first to commit original sin, not sex but gaining knowledge about sex.

If you don't want to read about one of the natural facts of human sexuality, lovemaking, perhaps you will want to take a vacation of sorts and skip this discussion. I don't think I will offend you; there's nothing here you don't know, but you might wish to avoid acknowledging your thoughts and knowledge, in which case it would be like observing an iceberg. It's okay to see the top twenty-five percent of the frigid waste; keep hidden the seventy-five percent that's undercover (or with an iceberg, underwater).

So, if you're still with me, let's begin with an observation: humans, as far as we know, are the only creatures that have intercourse face to face. And praying mantises are the only creatures we know which kill their mates, the female biting off the head of the male after copulation, and male bees (drones) die after mating with the queen, and Pacific (not Atlantic) salmon die after depositing their sperm and eggs.

How are these facts related, you ask? They aren't, unless you're a lover who has been rejected after a single episode of lovemaking, in which case you might have some sympathy for the male mantis or the salmon or the sacrificial drone. I point out the salmon and the bees and the mantises to make the point that sex is not love, not even affection, but a primitive drive whose only purpose is reproduction of the species.

That does not include the human whose sexual drive includes the need to reproduce but which is by no means limited to reproductive needs.

Face to face sexual intercourse is an evolutionary development, a male/female anatomical development involving the pelvis primarily but also the lower backbone.

Evolutionary developments, changes, are adaptations of some kind to some need. They don't happen overnight but over thousands of years. In evolution, it's adapt or die, and patience.

The evolving pelvis which permitted face to face

intercourse does not seem to have been a do or die need. Rather, it appears that pelvic evolution was simply part of the skeletal evolution as early human types began walking upright, the smaller, centered pelvis and backbone better able to support the entire upper body.

If that is so, then face to face sex was a happy byproduct (a modern judgment), a casual discovery.

Homo erectus, neanderthalensis or homo sapien- -who discovered frontal sex? We don't know. Somewhere along the evolutionary line our biological cousins did, and the world of human sexual practices changed forever.

The female became more than the receiver of the male's sperm; she became an active participant in the sex act. There was not one position for successful mating but many. The female could assume a dominant position. The male could stimulate not only the vagina but other erogenous areas of the woman's body simultaneously. Excitement and satisfaction became more than physical; humans could look into their partner's eyes and see on their partner's face sexual clues.

And somewhere along the way, human sex became less for procreation and more for pleasure. Humans are the only species in which the female has orgasms, an evolutionary development the beginning of which probably is unknown forever. Not only do females have permanent breasts, somewhere again along the evolutionary track they became sexual zones in addition to being feeding stations. Human evolution seems to have wired the breasts to the vagina, a human psychological factor as well as a physiological fact. The female became sexually receptive full time. The male did not have to wait for the female's "season." The female's reproductive period went from a brief monthly period of a few receptive hours or days to a monthly period of a few days when she was not reproductively receptive, and in modern woman that period of time is growing shorter.

And when the female learned to receive sexual pleasure, she was always "in season," physically if not emotionally. Emotional (spiritual, if you will) and physical (carnal) sex at this level are inseparable.

We'll never know the final truth, of course, but my guess is that the roots of what we call love and partnership and family can be traced in part to the evolutionary repositioning of the pelvis and the evolution of the sex act from the single purpose of depositing sperm to the multiple purpose of pleasure and release of passion--with no reproductive thoughts whatsoever.

Face to face lovemaking, as I see it, brought into focus the emotional or spiritual cords which bound two people together. Whether that first happened ten thousand years ago or fifty thousand years ago, we don't know. We do know that human types were mating tens of thousands of years ago. We also know that my logic about face to face intercourse helping to give birth to emotional male/ female ties might only be a fanciful leap of logic. There's no proof.

Yet I dare claim that the ability to have sex face to face, together with all the resulting factors I have mentioned, is true.

So what?

So three things. First, sex is natural, and rather than be denied, sexual conduct is deserving of attention.

Second, and very important for this discussion, sex is too important an element of love to be treated carelessly or crudely and for expressions of sex to be for the hurried release of physical tension.

And, third, loving sex is more than intercourse. For seniors, intercourse may not be an option. But the giving and receiving of sexual pleasure is a must. Repeat: the giving and receiving of physical sexual contact is a must.

I should repeat that a third time. A loving couple, no matter how elderly they might be, through trial and error and experimentation, must find satisfying ways to physically express their bond. It might be with stroking, the sensual caressing of the body and limbs; it might be by kissing not only the lips but other parts of the body; it might be by rubbing one's body against the other's; it might be by holding hands and hugging.

It must happen. Some form of intimate body contact must be made and sustained for a mutually satisfying period of time. A morning kiss on the back of the neck, an afternoon hug, an evening of entwined limbs--whatever-- is essential. The physical must be expressed in some meaningful way.

I dare say that the emotional undergirdings of love will not reach their full potential without the physical manifestation of that love.

That's one happy consequence of face to face lovemaking. Rub, kiss, touch, hug, hold, whatever is best, is done face to face, and face to face, one can speak the loving words that must accompany the touch and hug.

Elsewhere I write about the spiritual aspect of love. By emphasizing the physical I am not shortchanging the spiritual. They go hand in hand, and that's nature's fact.

She Used to Say. . . .

She used to say
that as a babe
I liked the breast,
and in the next breath
she'd tell her lack
of milk and how
from three weeks on
I was special fed.

I never knew
or remembered
which truth was true,
only that your breast
whenever seen
does have appeal,
and like a babe,
I would rest there.

Spooning

As two spoons tucked into a velvet pouch,
they lay, his front to her back.
Exhausted from their passion, they nested,
he between the roundness of her buttocks,
one hand cupped over welcoming breast.
That way they slept.

Always, following the sweet flush of their
fresh seasons' embraces,
they lay as such, two remaining as one.
Their coupling over, it was incomplete
without the snuggling, the pairing, the
front to back sleep.

It became the natural position
of repose, of nightly sleep.
In time, when passions mellowed to less
carnal demonstrations of oneness,
still they spooned, their nocturnal posturing
comfort and strength.

Through a lifetime of nights they remained
as two spoons in their cocoon
of elongated touch. Positioned so,
they spoke silently of fears overcome,
of hurts soothed, of joys to come, of love
year after year.

The Sight of Her

Not table flat,
but flat enough,
my land where roots
were old and deep.
She from august
mounts and valleys
enigmatic,
a wholesome land
undulating
like a winsome,
graceful maiden.
To flat land boy
the mounds and gaps
are seductive
revelations.
She just doesn't
understand why
the sight of her
is so much joy
for the little boy
from flat land sand.

Love's Enemies

The enemies of love are lovers.
They don't understand
that in the midst of what's grand
are the seeds of better and worse.
Love dies; it has to be reborn each day,
each hour, each minute, each second.
Love is conceived in love;
love is rebirthed by love,
love is proved with love.
Love dies when ignored;
love is stilled when voiceless;
love is lost when unused.
The death of love is love now and then,
a reward; withheld, punishment.
Love me tonight is not good enough.

Is It Sex or Love? Learning to Love

All the old backyard jokes to the contrary, for all species that mate for reproductive purposes (and for the human, for pleasure), the act of sexual intimacy comes naturally. It isn't learned; it's built into the historic, ancient memory of the species, whether mayfly or human.

Sex, the act of mating, is pretty much as old as life, take away a few million years when life reproduced by cell division and when life forms were hermaphroditic (both male and female) and could have successful reproductive sex with themselves or with another of the same species of either gender.

Having sex is all species' survival mechanism. No impregnating sex, no offspring. And for almost all species, sex (mating) is without further interest in the mate of the moment. In the insect and animal worlds, most males and females are notoriously promiscuous; they simply want the best eggs and the most virile sperm.

There are virtually no exceptions; some bird species come to mind in which pairing is long term with apparent fidelity, but even for monkeys and apes which live together in social groups, as do many species, sex is not limited to one partner.

Except for a few birds as noted, only the human has evolved sex into a pairing that lasts beyond the mating need, and that evolution is social, not biological. For all the anthropological and archeological evidence uncovered about humans, none reveals thoughts and intimate social behavior. At best we infer from the evidence at hand. No skull or fossil remains tell us what the early human was thinking.

We do know, and by inference push our assumptions

back in time, that with language the humans gave sex an extensive vocabulary, naming body parts and functions. Nouns, verbs, adverbs, and adjectives, many of them crude and derogatory, barnyard and barroom talk, define human sex.

But also, lost somewhere in human beginnings, we developed a vocabulary for those relationships which went beyond and/or transcended the sex act.

It's a very long leap of human development and social evolution to the age in which humans transformed sex into more.

Taking that leap, we might ask: when did sex become love? Here I'm using love as a generic word incorporating all the emotions and behavior we assign to it.

And the answer is, sex never did become love. Sex, mating for procreation or pleasure, is sex. Sex and love are not synonyms. In fact, they may have little in common, as any prostitute would tell you. Or any active "butterfly" or "mattress surfer" who flits from one lover to another.

Take one more leap with me. One doesn't have to learn how to have sex; one has to learn how to love. Sex is biological; love is social. Both the biological and the social evolve. Love is a social value evolving out of a biological function, i.e., fidelity to one's sexual partner.

(While the physical act of sex may be natural if inept and clumsy, satisfactory and fulfilling sex is learned. One learns how to please and how to be pleased, transforming sex into a meaningful, prolonged exchange of feelings far deeper and more important than the sex act by itself.)

Sex is sex and love is love whether you're twenty or eighty; really, there's no such thing as "senior" love or "senior" sex. What separates seniors from juniors is the experience accumulated with one's years. Whether we've learned anything because of our greater experience is questionable, not to demean experience and the one with greater experience but to point out what we already know: when it comes to love, in a very real sense, we are all beginners.

And we're all individually unique, because whatever it is we feel, it is our feeling alone. Others have had similar experiences and felt like emotions, but not ours. There's a commonality of shared feelings, but it's I (or you) who respond to love or its lack; it's the individual who feels the way he or she does, the one who suffers and accepts the risks and who is or is not rewarded by love's blessing.

Age has nothing to do with anything concerning love, nor does gender. We may, because of cultural causes, behave differently outwardly, but the inner emotions are similar even if expressed differently.

The most familiar and universal human theme is the love of a woman for a man, a man for a woman. That love is implied in the genesis story of three major religions, Judaism, Christianity and Islam. Love is the genesis theme of numerous so-called primitive religions, the love of the moon for the sun, for instance. Most beginning myths contain some element of love.

Carl Jung was not writing about love but about old age and death when he wrote, "The afternoon of human life must have a significance of its own and cannot be merely a pitiful appendage to life's morning." And from what or where derives that significance? Two sources, the nature of human life itself and the individual her or himself.

"Do we ever understand what we think," asks Jung? Not fully or really, because "there is a thinking in primordial images...older than historical man...outlasting all generations."

It seems to me that the very idea of love is one of those images, what Indian philosophy calls *kāma*. The human being carries within itself a basic love interest that is more than animal sex and pleasure (what Freud considered to be fundamental to all life, i.e., "sex and nothing but sex" and what some wag has called "sex a la carte," that is, the act of sexual gratification with no other thought than that).

The distinction between sex and love is important. Love is the greater concept, although surely its physical expression is of great importance. Carried within the concept of love is so much more: caring, committing, sharing, helping, doing, easing, and a lexicon of ideals which not only imply more than physical sex but which are practiced by those in love.

There are love images expressed from as far back as we know that are not merely descriptive sex, although there is that, and which transcend the purely physical and elevate love feelings to cosmic and spiritual heights above body parts and their functions.

The truth of love is ancient; it goes beyond the pornographic; it expresses itself in tenderness, shared comfort, mutual hopes, the future, togetherness, partnership. Love is more than a one night roll in the hay; it is forever. It is "in sickness and in health...until death do us part." Love is the pledge of fidelity. Love is "knowing" in the Biblical sense, and it is knowing the hopes and aspirations of the one loved. And it has been since human time began. From long ago, we carry the mosaic of such images within us; it is part of our humanity.

Having said all that, learning to love is a life-long process. We have to learn how to share, how to express caring, how to move from the individual self to partnership, how to forgive, how to reaffirm that closeness is more than sex, how to encourage one's mate, how to be bonded together and yet how to provide space so that each can grow as an individual.

So much to learn; so hard to learn, especially if role models were not present or parents were abusive or a former relationship was without love.

Seniors especially know where they failed to learn how to love or failed to practice what they had learned. Many second unions are stronger than the first because the partners are wiser; they work harder at loving and proving their love.

Loving does not come naturally, not as sex does. Sex is for the moment; love is for the long haul--assuming, of course, one has a longer view.

If what you offer is for the purpose of getting sex, you may be disappointed, just as you may be if you give sex as a reward for a past or future something. Among humans for whom sex is more than for perpetuating the race, sex's rightful place has been elevated to the physical and emotional expression of the union. At its best, sex becomes an extension of the love expressed, its meaning far exceeding the biological release of tension and/or frustration. The meaning of sex is found within the union itself.

"We don't make love (have sex) anymore." Anything I write here risks being a gross oversimplification. There might be lots of reasons why physical intimacy is not practiced. One, for the purpose of this discussion, is that love is lacking, or if love is present, that sexual practices have not been incorporated into that love beyond the mere sex act.

"It's not about sex," a man or a woman might say. "We're beyond all that."

Right away they had my unspoken sympathy. Their difficulties might not be about the act of sex, physiologically speaking, but a warning flag had been raised.

Often what was being said was, "We have no way or we have rejected all ways of expressing intimacy." The tender touch, the loving kiss, the meaningful hug had been banned from the relationship. Except for a word now and then, there's no physical expression of emotion--and without some honest, deeply meant demonstration of the love emotion, in time the basic emotion itself is denied.

Two contrary examples. I had known an elderly couple for two decades. We were friends within a larger circle of friends. Both of the older couple became ill, the wife dying a couple of years before her husband.

One day when I visited them, a nurse suggested I take the husband for a ride. "He needs an hour away," she said.

In the car the man told me, "Do you know I made love to her everyday? I miss that closeness and reassurance."

After a while I said, "You still can, you know."

"Oh, no! She's too sick for that!"

"You misunderstand. Do you hold her hand, cuddle with her, kiss her neck, say your loving words?"

Months later, after his wife had gone, he thanked me. "For what?" I asked.

"For telling me how I could make love to my wife. What you said was true. We expressed love to the end."

The second example is also an elderly couple. They were, as the British like to put it, "Past it."

The old man had had a very long marriage to a woman who, I must tell you, prided herself on her frigidity, claiming every physical manifestation of affection was a duty a wife hated but reluctantly performed. The man deserved some kind of sainthood.

The old woman he married after the passing of his first wife never had been married. Her mother had died early on and the woman took over her mother's chores, taking care of her siblings and for his long life, her father.

The marriage of which I speak lasted ten years, until

the old man's death. After the funeral, the widow said to those within hearing, "We managed because I made one rule (Actually, she was a tartar with many rules.). Each morning we'd greet each other with a kiss; each night we'd say goodnight with a kiss."

It was a good rule. However else they expressed love, the morning and evening kisses started and ended each day with an affirmation of love.

It's hard to stay mad with someone who touches or hugs or kisses you, reaffirming your high place in his/her universe. The physical expression, however simple and mundane it appears, soothes pain and hurt. The hug encourages even in failure; the kiss ennobles even in defeat; the touch strengthens when weak.

No, it is not about sex. It is about something broader and deeper. It is about love.

It's been suggested my view is too idyllic. I get the criticism even if idyllic is the wrong word. An idyll is a brief romantic interlude (and I certainly don't mean brief here) in a rustic country setting. The better word is to accuse me of idealism, seeing things as they might be rather than what they are. Love is love and sex is sex, my critics say, and never shall the twain meet.

That attitude has been around forever. One expression of it is the old saw, "women give sex to get love; men give love to get sex." And I admit there is abundant evidence for the pejorative thought.

On the other hand, there is overwhelming evidence that most couples sincerely want to include sex in their love but that they want their love to be more than sexual. Such couples, consciously or unconsciously, work at maintaining and strengthening their love bonds--and most of those bonds go beyond sexual intimacy.

The love of two people, one for the other, is not

built into the race. We possess some intimations of what goes into a partnership, but for the most part everything is learned. A union is trial and error, learning what pleases and what displeases. When errors are learning trials, there is forgiveness, another attitude learned. There is give and take, and both require patience. There's no need to catalog what's involved. You know them as well as I do.

Learning to love and to be loved has rewards surpassing the sexual. Remember, a union however defined is for the long term, forever, we pledge. Love provides us with a friend, a companion, a partner, a helpmate, in one person. Love is someone to soothe troubled brows, share pain, give courage. Love is reaching for the stars guided by someone who loves you. Love is giving strength to the one you love.

Willa Cather, the American novelist, was correct. There are only two or three factual or fictional human themes, and they are played over and over again as though they are brand new. Actually, I can count four: great journeys, great discoveries, heroes and heroines, and romance. Many themes overlap. It may be that your life journey is profoundly romantic or that your heroic role model made significant discoveries.

What I'm driving at is that love of one person for another is an ancient theme which each of us acts out as though it was original with us. Creatures have been walking ever since life crawled out of the seas, yet each of us has to learn to walk. Likewise, learning to speak and read and write. So giving love has to be learned, just as receiving love has to be learned. Love as something more and deeper than sex is not built into the human species; it is a value achieved by learning and a value strengthened by practice. Its rewards are countless.

If I seem to be making an issue of this it is because,

whether junior or senior, each time one falls in love it is like beginning again. Seniors are a bit wiser but they are literal beginners. The sexual aspect as an event comes more or less naturally. All the other aspects of love, amour, are not built into our genes. Anyone in love would be well served remembering that.

Naked Truth

I wanted to take off her clothes,
lovingly, like a gourmet cook
peels an onion, layer after layer,
to find the freshness there
beneath the outer, false covers.
I wanted to see the whole of her,
not to slice and dice and cook
in love juice but to see
her ungarmented and unguarded,
the essential nakedness
shorn of lies or pretense or illusion.
Naked, there is no shield;
she is what her body is,
fresh, uncomplicated, aware
that I not only see her, I see into her.

Mute Metaphor

White mute swans make my pond their home.
They ignore me; I don't ignore them; in fact,
I envy them, their color pure, their fidelity certain,
their ritual water dancing in spring love
(least I choose to suppose it so),
their paired water glide effortless.
That last I see as a metaphor.
Beneath the fascinating ripples of their swimming
their feet are paddling like mad. Pairing takes hard work;
dancing on the water's surface takes hard work;
preening is hard work, and I wonder if their fidelity
takes as much work and if they're white because white
is the color of purity. That thought, I decide,
is inglorious. Black swans are faithful, too, although
no black swans glide and love and mate on my pond.
Mute swans are voiceless, their arguments unheard.
They are pugnacious, quick to attack without cause.
They share my pond with me; I am not welcome
to share my pond with them, their selfish trait.
They tolerate certain ducks and Canada geese
and seagulls that aren't even birds of a feather.
But they are handsome or beautiful, however one measures
their welcome appearance. I forgive them their faults
(by human standards) in exchange for their grace
and for their faithfulness to their mate.

Your Name

Spell joy;
spell love;
spell happiness;
spell hopes and dreams,
and wonder
and a host
of other words
that flood the mind.
Each, having
singular
meanings, is spelled
only one way;
each contains
your precious name.

But What Makes a Love Poem?

The easiest way to answer the question may be the least satisfactory, but try this. If you or I write something and call it a poem, as far as I'm concerned, it's a poem. Others may not think so, but that's their opinion. You and I are the authors, so we can call something a poem if we want to, hiding behind William Carlos Williams, "a poem is a small (or large) machine made of words," and with those words it's not what we say as much as what we make from the words.

Using that logic, a love poem is what it is because we say so. Take the poem "Criticism" as an example. There's not a love word anywhere within its ten lines. The opening line, "Criticism should float down like feathers," is really about love talk. So is the line, "Speak with care, softly." That's love's way. "Bellicose prose that cuts to hurt" is not.

Love is a huge emotion, and wrapped within it is everything we are and do. Simple poems about squeezing toothpaste tubes and automobile driving are part of, albeit tiny parts, of the whole. The little bits sometimes demand more attention than the great big thoughts.

Love is joy. It is agony when it fails. To write about the pain of lost love, then, is to write about love. What we have lost, how we experience love's absence, what we project from our failure tells us something about love, too. As a matter of fact, we may not know fully the essence of love until we have lost it.

Calling a poem a love poem does not end the author's responsibility. I offer what I call love poems, my verbalized feelings, my success and failure, my joy and my pain, my hope filled dreams and my disappointment. Love has two faces, love that is realized and love that fails. Sometimes love does not work out the way one hopes. Sometimes it dies; sometimes it's weak and doesn't last; sometimes it's betrayed; sometimes it simply was not meant to be. Cupid with his gold and lead arrows often is capricious when shooting them.

There are numerous collections of love poems and each may contain poems or lines of poems worth remembering. But they are not my lines or my feelings or my intimate, personal experiences. Unlike the young girl I mentioned previously, I don't want to use others' experiences, suggesting they are mine, and unlike the mockingbird, I don't want to mimic someone else. My feelings are unique because they are mine; therefore they should be expressed in my own words.

I've read meaningful love poems and silently have thanked the author for saying something and/or feeling something that reflected my situation. That's what good poetry does: it says for you or remembers for you or draws a picture for you, the poet sharing through his or her experience, and thus seeming to know the nature and depth of your feelings, words you would speak if you could. I wrote about that once in a poem, "The Poet's Best," and from that poem I quote myself.

> ...poets
> strive to find the rhythms
> of life, that in our lined words
> readers find self vignettes,
> images of places, people,
> feelings the reader knew
> once and recollects.
> "Yes, yes, that's what I knew and felt."
> "You know, I've been there."
> "The joy, the sorrow; they were mine."
> "In that word land I dwelt,
> but could not express

what was in my mind and heart."
"You have said it for me."
The poet seeks that success.

When I write poetry, it is first of all for myself, to see if I can put in lines and on paper the thought I have. I'm really talking just to myself. Then I decide whether I want to share it and with whom. Some of these poems were shared only with a special individual, many have never been read by anyone.

Somewhat reluctantly, I have decided to share my poetic thoughts with a larger audience. I do so hoping the poems will be meaningful to the reader in some way. I always am aware that my words of feeling are not yours. I wish you would write your own words, whether of a love that will last throughout eternity or about a love that ended all too soon. Sharing joy and happiness or sharing pain and sorrow, there are those who need someone to write their feelings, just as you might seek some lines here that reflect yours.

One day I remarked to an editor who was reading some of my poetry that I had thrown away more poems than I had saved. She was reading a poem she disliked. "Structure good; phrasing good; idea stinks," she announced. Naturally, I wondered about her qualifications.

"Poetry is like cooking an old rooster," she continued, misusing an old joke. "You put the rooster and a brick into the same pot, boil them for two days, and then throw away the rooster and eat the brick." She paused. "Maybe you threw away the bricks."

I think wherever she is she's still laughing. What I don't know is if she is laughing with me or at me. Later she read other poems and her only reaction was a quiet "yes."

She wrote "nature" poems, buttercups and maple leaves turned gold and scarlet, lily-of-the-valley and johnniesthat-jump-up, that kind of garden/nature image that only if you knew her would reveal her inner truth:

> We tend the roses
> with more care
> than we tend
> our garden of love.

My words, not hers, but her thought. I told her once, when I was a kid, we'd hold buttercups beneath our chins, and if the buttercup yellow was reflected there, we loved someone. Then we were supposed to tell who.

She'd never heard of that children's game. Once when I saw her at a reading of her poetry, she told me she had tried the buttercup. She couldn't see if the buttercup was reflected on her lower chin. She asked her husband to look. He reported nothing showed. "Too bad," she said, "I wanted to tell him after all these years for whom the buttercup shined."

That's a real poet. I didn't, but since I knew her husband quite well, I wanted to kick his butt. He had been offered a sublime moment of affirmation and had not recognized it.

Write it, I told her. She never did; I don't know if she ever tried. After she died, I tried the buttercup theme.

> The children play.
> "Secret, secrets," they yell.
> "Who's secret to tell?
> Who'll tell us secrets today?"
>
> Childhood secrets
> don't remain secrets long,
> the urge to tell strong,
> better than playing pirates.

"I'll tell you what.
Buttercup, buttercup!
Bring your chin close up.
Come on, boys, let's see...."

I never did finish the poem. I knew what I wanted to say; I didn't know how to say it, that the feelings of love are secret, that childhood secrets become adult secrets, that the buttercup test might be childish but that there are other tests, that unless love is reflected upon two, it fails.

The Toothpaste Tube Caper

Properly chastised, I,
miserable miscreant
and confirmed coward,
took the high road,
confessed the erroneous act
and begged forgiveness.
What else to do?

But I had learned from her:
one does not seek forgiveness,
one plots sweet revenge.

The toothpaste tube,
middle squeezed indeed!
In secret, sneaky pleasure,
I strangle mid tube,
sneer at fate and her ire,
and squeeze again,
from the bottom,
filling the telltale offending gap,
a furtive display
of independence.

A Sad Choice

I don't know for whom
I feel more sorrow,
you who had so much
love to give
and couldn't
or I who longed
to receive it
and didn't.

Driving to Endanger

With one good eye
and that not too good,
it's best to keep
one eye on the road.
The question is,
whose good eye is best?
    "Too close!" "Slow down!"
    "Gas it!" "Close him out!"
    "Don't let him pass!"
    "Didn't you see the light?"
Hell's bells, my love,
I can't see the white line.
    "Want me to drive?
    "I'm better than you."
No argument;
the glove compartment
holds the tickets;
none of them are mine.

Love School Lesson # 3

It should be clear in certain cases,
and if not, touch all the bases.
One of the first things taught in love school:
never come between the one you love
and his or her lovers.
Such adolescent behavior spoils
your own affair, and such trouble boils
a lovers' stew. You, he/she, a third
or fourth mix, back alley bouillabaisse,
not pure white vichyssoise.
As a lover, you must know your place
in your loved one's hierarchy. Face
the truth and be content with that;
you're the lover he/she comes home to,
but you're not number one.
"That's the way it is," he/she will say.
"That's what I am. I am yours today.
Tomorrow? Well, tomorrow we'll see.
I might go away. I'll think of you.
I do love you, you know."

Friends and Lovers

"...friendship is the sweetest form of love," claims Ann Gottlieb. It's hard to find fault with such a tender sentiment, and her statement does have a ring of truth. But I'm inclined to turn the thought around: love is the deepest form of friendship.

It's not simply a matter of semantics. Love, lovable, adorable (originally a religious word), amorous, and other words have a variety of meanings. In keeping with the use of the word "love" in *Seniors in Love,* the love word here is of the French "amour" with its emotional and physical connotation.

Thus friendship as "the sweetest form of love" does not (although it can) imply a sexual meaning. Usually, friends are not "in love" and are not lovers.

To turn Gottlieb's statement around, as I have done, "love is the deepest form of friendship," implies a conscious level of amour plus--the plus being the friendship amour does not always imply.

It's possible to be a friend without being a lover, just as it's possible to be a lover without being a friend. It is not possible, I think, to have a meaningful and lasting love affair if there is not present also great friendship. Friends and lovers. "He/she is my husband/wife; he/she is my best friend" sums up the ideal partnership.

I was told once, "All my best friends are women," by a woman whose marriage was floundering. "I never share my feelings with my husband; he wouldn't understand."

"Wouldn't understand what?"

"It's a female thing. You wouldn't understand."

Not knowing what it was I wouldn't understand, she was correct up to a point. If she withheld her thoughts and feelings from her husband, he couldn't understand either.

How many times has a man or a woman said, "If you don't know, I'm not going to tell you."? Defeat and failure are in the air.

The woman I mention assumed the failure of her husband's understanding and thus used that assumption as the excuse for her conduct (and misconduct). While she dismissed my help quickly, on two occasions she attended a group session to which, by the way, she was not invited. Unfortunately for her, the group's focus was not on marital issues. That group was for men and women who were seeking ways of overcoming shyness in group settings. Most of the members of that group were people who suffered from low self esteem and/or verbal and social inadequacies born of that image.

Not so the woman in question. She took the opportunity to speak about her marriage and her unable-to-understand husband. The gist of her statements were consistent: she and her husband were not friends, did not do very much together, had few common interests, took separate vacations, and fought over nothing at all. They lived together but as two separate entities.

I didn't know her husband, but I was beginning to understand his lack of understanding, and quite contrary to certain ethical norms, I was glad when she gave up on the group, after accusing the several bewildered participants of their lack of understanding.

Frankly, I think most of them understood some of her "problem." They weren't able to sympathize with so jaundiced and self-centered an individual.

My insight into the whole tiny episode was 1) I was never going to be able to help her had she continued with me, and 2) her existence was devoid of friendship, either with her husband or with others she mentioned, because they were to blame. For what, I wasn't sure. For everything, I guess.

That woman had many issues. For this discussion one stands out: her lack of marital friendship. Nothing in common, separate vacation, etc. might be a symptom or might be a cause. Or both. Not being the friend of your mate or partner is indicative of a coming marital failure. I suspect the failure had happened, the couple living out their lives together but miserable.

I believe in saving relationships, rebuilding marriages or unions beginning with the love that once was present. I also believe that if a couple cannot work at saving their partnership, or won't work at it, they should end it. Most of the damage has been done, and if there is no damage control, the union or marriage may be more destructive than separation and/or divorce.

I'd be hard pressed to find a reason for continuing a marriage if the couple refuse to be friends. I'm opposed to marriage in the first place if friendship is absent.

A contemplated marriage/union/relationship or rebuilding a relationship begins with friendship, the (re)discovery of common interests, common goals, a sense of adventuring into the unknown together, mutual support, the pledge of working hard to make a go of the relationship. And with the woman in question, being faithful. There are good things, usually, upon which to build. And there's a lot of junk to be discarded. And forgiveness to be given and received.

Friends (and lovers) either forgive their partner's faults or they learn to forgive. Friends (and lovers) agree to disagree, and find ways to creatively and ethically compromise. Friends show friendship by being a friend. Lovers first show love by being a friend.

If friendship is absent, love cannot follow. More than

once I've heard a variation of "I'm in love with him/her but I'm not sure I like him/her."

Oh, oh. The "I'm not sure" indicates a failed or lack of friendship and a deep doubt or mistrust of the one loved. It doesn't mean love is purely a physical love; it does mean that a foundation upon which to build is lacking. You cannot be friends with someone you don't like, and in the long term, you cannot love someone you wouldn't want as a friend.

Unfortunately for many might-be unions, there is a form of friendship that is exploitive. It is not friendship at all but uses the friend word to get or gain something with no intention of returning the favor. It is the kind of misnamed friendship that uses people, sometimes to the point of selfish abuse of other people's desire for true friendship and love.

Friendship and exploitation are mutually exclusive words. No way do they go together, yet maintaining a form of friendship just to gain something is all too common. And so is giving love (or, more properly, sex) as a reward for favors received. In an earlier day such a woman was called a paramour, a courtesan, a hussy; a man was called a rake, a wencher, a gigolo. It is alleged to be humankind's oldest profession.

But we are not talking about professionalism, only to make the point that friendship and love must be conjoined in sincerity if a loving relationship is to flourish.

A second issue raised often is the role of friends who are not one's romantic love interest. Sometimes this can be a very delicate and emotionally charged issue. One partner (or both) may have genuine friends of either or both sexes who are meaningful persons in that partner's life. There may be a long history of friendship and shared activities. Such friendships demand attention and sustenance; they should not be ignored or cast aside.

That they are continued and enjoyed takes skillful balancing. One makes a place for old friends in the new relationship, just as the new romantic interest accepts the old friends' place.

But what happens when an old friend demands more attention than the new love? When one's new love and one's old friend become competitors? When each is jealous of the other? And each wants more than equal time?

The lover and the friend never will reach an accommodation. It is the partner who has both friend and lover who must achieve a balance and who must make it clear to both the limits and the ranges of affection.

It's not unknown that the friend is a secret would-be lover. Even same sex friends. And if such a friend forces a choice, the outcome is not sure. Often the choice is of the friend, a long history overcoming an uncertain future. Here love does not prevail; a kind of practicality does. Since one cannot have both, one chooses the seemingly secure known rather than the possibly insecure unknown.

Both lover and friend have a responsibility before someone has to make a choice. A sincere lover makes room for the friend; a genuine friend makes a place for the loved one. In the best of all worlds, they become steadfast friends.

Most people have friends. Each friend is a wonderful part of one's life. What happens when some of your partner's friends are not liked by you or your friends are not liked by him/her?

Elsewhere and in *Seniors* I write about providing space for your partner, and here is a time and a place for space. Providing space means allowing, encouraging even, your loved one to pursue individual initiatives. A time with friends, even those you cannot stand, is such a time. It will have great meaning for your partner. Your own feelings aside, you will approve of his/her friendships. Not the least, it is a demonstration of trust.

However, when a friend becomes one's major confidant and one's mate is not considered worthy of confidence, trouble is brewing. One's love and loving friendship may be blowing away, sometimes with no one being aware of it. There's woman-talk and man-talk, but if the talk is about one's union and about troubles within that union, the place for discussion is with one's mate. Talking with a friend who has a vested interest in you is muddying the water. If bad comes to worse, then skilled counseling is available--for both you and your partner. Friends who pose as amateur psychologists and who have their own agenda will, in the long run, make things worse, no matter how well-meaning they are.

Your love is too precious to put into the hands of friends, no matter how close they are and have been. Good and true friends will know the distinction between your friendship for them and your love for someone else. And they will know from their own experience that the best of all possible worlds is having a lover who is your best and closest friend. They might envy you; they will not be jealous of the one you love.

Guard well, then, your friends, and guard well your faithful lover who is, of all friends, your best friend.

The Affair

Our romance was meant for two,
and 'though it was but a fling,
remember this: I loved you
and for a while could sing
of lovebirds and red roses,
light and laughter, newness bright,
kissing and loving poses.
Dreams came true, and, oh, the sight
of you filled my heart and mind,
images of together,
loving, the romantic kind
upon which is built forever.
Little did I know that my lover
could never be, that beyond
the moment was another
waiting her chance to respond.
So quickly you let me go;
so soon I was of no use.
For loving you, naught to show
but your unexplained abuse
for wanting what never could
be offered and never would.

Sing a Song, My Dear

Sing,
sing a song, my dear,
sing for me.
Sing off key,
raspy voice,
misplaced beat,
I won't care, my dear.
Sing for me
songs of love.
Sing of faith,
sing of trust,
sing you care, my dear.
Angel's song
I will hear,
heavenly
melodies
true and clear, my dear.
Sing to me,
sweetheart, bring
harmony
to my life.
Sing. I hear you, dear.

On Children

Mary and Raymond (not their real names) just got married. I'm very pleased for them. I was not invited to their wedding, didn't expect to be. I know them only casually, fine, gentle, attractive people who seem well suited for the trials a late in life marriage of disparate ages creates. Raymond is twenty years older than Mary, but neither looks nor acts his age. Both have been without partners for several years, each living in his or her own spacious house.

I first heard of their engagement and planned marriage while I was having lunch with four of Raymond and Mary's neighbors. The table talk was positive, not always the case, and the difference in ages was mentioned briefly but without negative comment.

Three or four years earlier Raymond had sought the hand of another senior widow. That was common knowledge. What was interesting was the the luncheon table report that Raymond had dropped that woman. The woman in question always had suggested she dropped Raymond. Not that it makes any difference; Raymond and his former woman friend, attempting to save face, perhaps, reported recent history in diametrically opposite terms.

No one mentioned the fact that Raymond's and his former woman friend's children disliked and distrusted each other. Each set of children raised a fuss with their parent when they thought the parents might marry.

That marriage might have worked; it never had a chance, what with warring children and open hostility between children and their parent's "other." Raymond and his earlier love moved on to other people, Raymond to a lovely woman and a future wife.

What crossed my mind was how destructive of a

parent's future children can be. Raymond had a second chance for love and happiness tarnished by hostile children. Perhaps the children were right. Perhaps his earlier second chance at love was not in either parents' best interest. Yet parents allow (as if there is any choice) their children to take risks; so children must allow their parents to take risks. Fortunately, Raymond was given a third chance.

Raymond's first woman friend's children behaved the same; he was not a suitable match, harbored unsavory designs upon their mother's resources or was too old or too something. They had found fault with other suitors before and they would find faults again, and their mother would listen and believe the truth of the faults told her, even when she knew better. She likewise had other chances at love, but that's another story. There's no telling of the children's motivation.

On a different note, earlier in another piece, I said children couldn't spank their parents.

From my childhood on I wanted to do just that. My brother and I had no father, he having skipped out long before we ever reached public school age. I was five; my brother was three years younger.

In time there were a couple of men in our mother's life, one I had known since I could remember. He was a widower bringing up a son. The son was everything a stepbrother could be, and I had great affection for the father. I hoped he would become my father. My brother seemed to have similar thoughts.

It didn't happen. My mother never let any man get close to her. Even in later years, when I was in college, my brother and I would suggest, "Go for it." She didn't; neither my mother nor the man remarried, although they remained friends until his death.

I was never privy to my mother's thoughts. She

simply closed her mind to the possibility of loving a second time. I never asked about the failed (from my point of view) relationship. I knew enough to know it was none of my business.

Over the years I've met many people from similar situations. "I wish my mother had...." "I wish my father had...."

And I've heard the parent's side. "But what will the children think?" Sometimes that question is raised by someone who is considering living with but not marrying a new partner.

I always try to guide the parent toward his or her own answers. I refuse to judge the many issues involved, moral, religious or social.

In all honesty, most often I want to say, "Forget the children. This is your life we're talking about. What is right for you?"

As a matter of reality, children cannot be ignored entirely, but when grown children are involved, that's what they are, grown up adults, and how they view your relationships is up to them, not you. Unless there is an untoward moral or ethical issue, children will adapt to the facts of life and accommodate to your decision, loving you even if you do seem a bit wayward.

And if your decision turns out to be the wrong one, they will be there for you, just as you were and are there for them.

Most children want their single parent to be happy, even if they don't like the avenue the parent has chosen. Not all children are like those who began this piece. Thank goodness for that. I have no evidence to offer, but I do believe a happy, even if misguided, parent makes the children happy. And I do believe that most children end up saying, "She/he isn't all that bad," which today is about as high a compliment as one can hope to receive.

All I've written notwithstanding, it would be a mistake not to include your children in your thought processes somewhere along the way, although just where is a question. "I've found a man/woman who has become a very special friend." It doesn't have to be more, but even that simple statement will start the questions flowing. Before they do get asked, you should decide what you want to reveal and how much you want to tell. Not all, it's not show and tell, but enough so that should more than friendship develop, it will not come as a complete surprise.

By revealing a new relationship on whatever level, you are not asking for your children's approval but for their understanding and support.

If, and I have to emphasize the if, they are understanding, they will offer you support if not encouragement. Secretly, they may wonder if you are certifiably sane, but they will reverently hope and pray that your relationship works and that you will be the happy and fulfilled parent they hope for.

One plus in your favor is the effort you put into providing situations in which your children and your intended partner's interact. That's where we began this thought, and that's where we'll leave it. Children are not unreasonable; they just act that way sometimes, just like their parents.

This Time Should Be....

This time should be the sweetly
scented afternoon of our lives
when buttercup and daisy
rival the sun and apple orchards
glow with delight, when roses
add pink and white and scarlet red
and earth's perfumes fill the air,
when color is too much to bear
yet remains when eyes are shut,
pleasing, teasing all our senses.
This should be the wonder time
before twilight dims our sight
and evening dew dulls the senses.
This time should be the sweetly
remembered season of our lives.

Wealth and/or Love?

An elderly man I do not know married an elderly woman I know only by sight. We have never spoken.

"That old hen got married," a friend told me. "Having money can get you anything," another said. "But he's wealthy," said a third. "New money and old money: quite a combination," the first again.

I got to thinking. My friends saw wealth joined to wealth, the marriage of bank accounts, property and portfolios. In a thirty second conversation they had settled the matter and moved on to other world affairs, leaving me to think about a marriage about which I knew exactly nothing.

There's nothing quite so useless and senseless as thinking about something about which you haven't a single clue. Neither partner is particularly physically attractive. It's hard to be a fashion model when you're pushing eighty.

What he sees in her...what she sees in him...has to be within. My friends saw only fortunate, material trappings; they dismissed entirely the possibility that she loves him, he loves her.

In a material minded world, love does happen. Until it's proved otherwise, I'm going to believe that two older people I do not know found each other and love each other, and I'll envy them.

However, the matter of money and love often is not settled as easily as that. When people of means marry or become partners, however the union is achieved, money is not a problem. It might be an issue later, but sound prenuptial planning and agreements can successfully satisfy the concerns of both adults and their children.

But the potential union of individuals of unequal

wealth can be a major concern. One comes to the table, as it were, bearing few material gifts. If the other has substantial resources, there is an inequality of means and feelings of inadequacy that are hard to ignore.

The lesser (in financial terms) may feel inferior, unable to provide the life style his/her partner has lived. For seniors, there is no ship en route bearing a fortune. The lesser may feel inadequate, even a failure, his/her ego diminished.

The major resource holder may wonder if he/she is going to have to give up accustomed luxuries, or pay the bills, or be financially responsible for the partner.

Perhaps there will be sharing of pooled amounts determined in large measure by the amount the lesser can contribute to the pool. What does the major resource person do with his/her surplus? How use it? For one? For both? What happens when one child or another needs financial help? Does the woman help the man's child or he hers?

What happens to resources when illness or accident strikes? If they move into one or another's home, who owns what? I don't need to go on. The practical issues are obvious when one partner has substantially more than the other.

It is not simply a matter of money; it is a huge emotional hurdle. Suppose the male believes it is his responsibility to provide for the family, even if that family is but two, and discovers he cannot by himself. He is defeated by a serious blow to his ego. Or suppose the woman, to protect her future with no other motive, believes the male's resources should be used first before she contributes a portion to their common welfare. That's part of her security blanket. What then?

Love will find a way is a totally inadequate notion. Love will not find a way by itself. Love needs help, serious, well considered help, else love will turn to resentment--or worse.

I know love is supposed to be sweet talk and cooing. "We" and "our" are predominant words, but they don't mean "We're going to live off your money" or "All your wealth is going to become our wealth."

If love is present, if you, to make this personal, plan on a shared future, if you believe in a union of body and soul--and material resources--you have to get down to the hard, practical fiscal facts of your lives.

Cut the romance stuff. Deal with the reality.

One of the realities is "What's mine is mine." Perhaps you can live with that. If you can't, then you best have a second thought.

One of the realities is "I don't want to support you." Ditto above.

One of the realities is "I want...." and you can't provide. Ditto.

But suppose the two of you, so much in love, commit all you have to the union. Does that solve the problem? I don't think so. For good reason.

First, the loving thing to do is offer not only your self but your worldly goods. When wealth is unequal, I think that gesture is a mistake. You may mean it now; later you may not.

So there are limits, and love should be limitless. Call the limits ground rules. I don't know what they should be for you, common agreement about how you use the money you have in common, vacations, new car, whatever extraordinary expenses come with life. There's compromise in this. Be sure you don't compromise beyond your ability to live with the compromise.

Second, having worked out the major agreements, seek financial help from someone who deals with prenuptial matters. He or she will set before you scores of issues which if not resolved while you are lovy-dovy can be real trouble down the road.

Third, review your agreements from time to time. Nothing says they can't be modified to meet your and your mate's needs. Working out the practical realities in your union is, or should be, an act of love. You are then sharing your needs and the needs of your partner and sharing the solutions.

Fourth, pay attention to the ethics involved in compromise. Stupidly, compromise has been given a bad name. Compromise is essential to any marriage or union. It's more than mere give and take; it is finding the solution to a given issue that best serves the needs and goals of each. Yes, there is giving; yes, there is taking. That's personal in the sense we're speaking. The larger search is to maintain the foundation of the union itself, and that's greater than the individuals, each the sum of one; it is the sum of two, you and he/she. Emphasize the "and."

Fifth, in all things, behave with love. That's what brought you to this in the first place. Make love work for you. Sometimes love needs understanding, too. Figure out why you are together, figure out ways to stay together. If you are lucky enough to deal with unequal wealth and fortunate enough to create a meaningful compromise and wise enough to achieve agreeable guidelines, love one another.

Love needs your help to light the world you dreamed.

And if the issue of money looms too great, if there's no agreement, then realize that love does not conquer every time, that love does not solve all problems. Better to know that now than too late.

Love As Art

Our ancient ancestral people of ten, twenty thousand years ago were fascinated by the hand, and from Europe to Australia they drew its outline and filled in the colors.

Sometimes the hand wasn't drawn or painted; sometimes the hand was rubbed with ashes or talc or berry juice, and like a rubber stamp, made its mark on a stone or a cave wall. Sometimes hands of color were imposed one on top of an other.

Was the hand the first art object? Perhaps. Who knows. We know that the hand's image is very, very old, older than sketches of animals which hunters sought for meat or from which they sought escape.

Undoubtedly the ancients sought to leave a mark, a human impulse, I suppose, to say to someone, "I existed."

I've never understood why such marks, hand drawings and beasts and the like, are not considered art. Not until, tens of thousands of years later, when we come upon Ubaid, Sumerian, Mesopotamian, and, later, Egyptian and Chinese objects, do we begin to think in terms of art, and then we think in terms of decoration, a vase or a wall, or in terms of beliefs, art depicting deities and/or what such deities did for or to humans.

I'm intrigued by the hand. Why not a foot or lips? I suppose, again, because the hand did most everything. The amazing hand with its opposing thumb, long in use before the first hand was positioned and traced on a cave wall, was an instrument, all unconscious, to be sure, that built shelters and herded live stock and gathered vegetables and fruit and protected people. The hand was natural; what it did must have seemed like magic. It hunted meat and delivered babies. It carried fire and soothed a mate's brow. It said "I was here" and then pointed the way. It deserved special recognition.

It's a long way from primitive man (generic term) and his cave art, through stone and bronze and iron ages, to modern man. The wheel was an artistic representation of the sun; later it became a functional device. Stones knives and skinning tools were functional tools that became artistic creations that went beyond mere functionality.

Art has been with us for a long time. It expressed who we were as well as what we did and thought. Someone making a lance, for example, decided to decorate it with feathers or color dyes. It became the maker's expression of something he felt; something told him to make his lance unique. It was his mark. He had expressed his individuality. A woman formed a simple clay pot. The plainness drew her attention; she scratched lines and created a design. It pleased her. She had created a useful object, and decorating it, she had become an artist. A child carved random marks on a turtle shell, making the turtle his. Later he carved images in alabaster or limestone. He would be called an image-maker, and in some time and some place, he would have a special role. He would paint, carve, cast, and weave the human adventure.

With the hands, a high ranking professional artist and artisan or a man or woman sitting by the family fire, function and beliefs were given artistic form.

I don't want to pursue an art analogy very far; it would become tedious. Rather, I'm attempting to put you into a frame of mind to consider these thoughts.

The first is what Henri Matisse said of his art: it is "the expression of a dream which is always inspired by reality."

Matisse was influenced by the Frenchman, Henri Bergson, a confused and confusing philosopher. If I understand Bergson correctly, he said that images existed in two forms: a thing, a person, an event (reality) and your memory of the thing or whatever as it appears to you (image). A simple explanation would be the difference between an event (the reality) and your memory of that event (the image), what Matisse called dreams.

Thus whatever you are thinking about, or what the artist is painting, is not the reality but is your image or dream of that reality. And with Bergson, whatever you are dreaming about (your image of it) is always identified by the object itself.

Confusing? Who cares? Get on with it. Skip the double talk.

Okay, Let's cut directly to the idea that love and loving is an art. Dreams (images) are inspired by reality; they give us the courage to love, and love gives us the reason to dream.

Using Matisse's thought, the love dream emerges from the reality of being in love. Using Bergson's thought, the love dream is always about the one you love. Or to confuse you even more, setting Bergson and Matisse aside, the image of the trinity of beauty, light and love is our image of ourself and our loved one, a single image of spiritual unity.

But the reality is greater than either. The contemporary art historian and interpreter, Sister Wendy, provides us with a profound insight. She has said that the image behind all art is spiritual. That is, the image lifts us above and beyond our existent reality into a world of sublime emotional wonder. And least you think a nun is devoid of knowledge and appreciation of love, Sister Wendy includes the reality and image of human unions.

Because we love in a very complex world and because the love we share with another has universal (or at least earthly) ramifications and consequences, we cease being limited or constricted individual souls and become, by the sheer expansion of our egos, universal (or at least more inclusive).

So where does the art come in? In the artist's view, art is how we express (paint, perhaps) our reality. For us commoners, it's how we express to the one we love, verbally, with body language, through notes and letters and with flowers, the reality we perceive and the dream we have for both the present and the future with that loved one.

The expression of love is an art form. While the word love is an abstraction; the fact of love is a reality. There's no argument that the reality of being in love inspires great and wonderful dreams.

I've always envied the painter/sculptor artist. For all that goes into a piece of art, all the emotion, thought and skill, the viewer receives an immediate impression. It happens in a single moment. There's a flash of visual experience. Later, the viewer may study the painting or the sculpture closely and absorb its many facets, but what I envy is the ability to make that initial impression.

Not so the writer or the speaker. The reader/hearer must hold the book, turn the pages, listen, wait for something to happen. People discuss visual art and music; they argue with the written page or the spoken word. Perhaps you're doing that now. Each word becomes a challenge. Readers often are impatient or are looking for "the good parts." Listeners frequently are heard to say, "Get on with it."

So I will. Exhibiting love is part of the art; it's the whole picture you present to your partner, the big picture if you will, or the entire love experience you offer him/her, not unlike the movie concept of "the big screen."

But when the picture becomes too big, we can't take it all in all at once. When this happens the artist's skill is most apparent. The viewer, in this example your loved one, sees not one large canvas but an array of smaller areas of details:

how she or he is treated, the language used, emotional and physical responses, evidence of deep caring, displays of sharing, an infinite host of seemingly irrelevant items. When comfort is not offered, for instance, it clashes with love words, and the larger painting is smeared if not destroyed. When "me" is painted in large letters from frame to frame, the canvas is ripped, perhaps irreparably damaged.

There will never be a perfect picture. We all make mistakes or are careless. Sometimes we don't even know we have splattered a drop of paint on an otherwise lovely scene and that such carelessness and/or crudeness needs correcting.

The truth about painting your love picture is that it can't be completed alone; someone has to inspire you and then help you fill in the colors, give your impressions substance. The one you love, if you are loved, paints beside you, and what you finally produce is the work of two. Divine collaboration, if you're lucky enough to share in it.

As in the world of painting, some brush strokes will be grand and broad, others will be mini-dots. All the colors of the rainbow will be present, and so will black, because life has its dark moments. What you paint, what you and your partner paint, will be what you are and what you dream of becoming, realism and surrealism blended on the surface of your lives.

We must go to sculpture to add the third dimension to our art, the back side, the other side of the moon. You and your partner must work on that side, too, for the whole of you is both front and back, present and past, present and future. How do we know a ball is really round until we see its other side? It's not a philosophical question. We must know the whole of a thing, a person, ourselves, if we are to know what a thing or a person is and what we are.

And what our love is, the whole of it, with nothing

hidden, within every part of it, awaiting our sculpturing touch.

The artist's hand is no less, and the lover's hand is more. How you paint your life of love is a small matter; what you paint is everything. When your beloved stands back and views your colors, what will she/he see?

A good life painting will recount shared experiences, exchanged words of love, pledges of comfort and fidelity. And it will be good.

A grand painting will picture all that but with one addition: your grand painting will project into the future. To say "We were here" is meaningful. To say "We are going there, wherever there is, together" is sublime.

Which leads me to the second thought. It has to do with Auguste Rodin's sculpture, "The Kiss," the sensual (and sexually suggestive) embrace of two lovers. Emerging from the marble from which they were carved, their physical union is eternal. Rooted in the ancient stone, the sculpture will last as long as earth lasts. In my mind, it is one of the great artistic expressions of human love.

Among the literature about the sculpture in the Musée National Auguste Rodin in Paris, an unnamed critic is quoted as saying it is "the impossible union of souls by their bodies."

The "impossible" word is that critic's awe that from cold stone could emerge such moving figures, that within the reality of the stone was such an image and that from the image (dream; see above) could be created another lasting reality.

From the distant past when someone left a hand print on a stone wall to a Rodin sculpture may not seem to be well connected. But for the love artist the connection is immediate.

From ancient beginnings are the expressions of the

self, first the hand and later what that hand can create, from the individual self to the self which is not complete without another self, from a single body part, the hand, to the union of two bodies, from the physical union to the "union of souls."

Fanciful? Romantic? Both. That's what art produces: the dreams. The true art of love is taking the reality of love and creating greater images of love and from love dreams dreaming greater dreams.

Rodin's figures embrace. It is a moment of reality frozen forever. And it portrays the image, the dream of more. The kiss is passion and in the passion is promise. The realist, I suppose, sees only the promise of a more intimate embrace. The dreamer sees that and beyond that. The dreamer sees what the critic saw, the profound spiritual union of the lovers' souls.

Be a dreamer.

Lyrics: Yesterday's Song

They played our song yesterday,
a song of love and light;
they played our song yesterday
and made a bad day bright.

The song was sung the old way,
the way it used to be;
they sang the song just the way
you used to sing for me.

I heard you sing yesterday;
you sang again to me.
I know you sang just to say
that you remember me.

The song came from years long past,
yet fresh as morning dew;
like the dew, it didn't last,
unlike memories of you.

The song came from other days;
the thought of you brought light.
How treasured our yesterdays
through songs I still recite.

A Love Poem: Fact or Fiction?

When the poet writes love poems, are they fact or fiction?

Does it matter?

What's the poet doing, anyway?

Shakespeare said it: "That man that hath a tongue, I say, is no man, / If with his tongue he cannot win a woman." That line of four hundred years ago from "Two Gentlemen of Verona" is chauvinistic in the extreme. Not only does it exclude women from the thoughtful, intellectual, linguistic universe, it implies that women are so weak as to be receptive to any word a superior man might utter. At the very least, the same should be said of women.

Not excusing Shakespeare's cultural chauvinism, there is a hidden germ of truth. Some poetry is a man's or a woman's tongue of love.

From the same play, Shakespeare said, "They do not love that do not show their love." Thus, "If you're in love, show me!...If you're on fire, show me!" to use words from Frederick Loewe and Jay Lerner's song "Show Me." And for the poet and the would-be poet, that means write it as well.

Of course, Shakespeare also had King Lear say, "My love's / More richer than my tongue." We certainly hope so. In other words, no matter the words, they never will do justice to the feelings which gave them birth.

What about the other side of love, the love that failed, what Elvis Presley's words meant: "...since my baby left me / ...I've found a new place to dwell / ...it's down at the end of a lonely street / At Heartbreak Hotel." Or as Hal David and Burt Bacharuch expressed it: "One less egg to fry.... / No more laughter, no more love / since he went away," in "One Less Bell to Answer."

What the poet is trying to do is convey a feeling. The feeling may be one of joy or one of sorrow. It may be a feeling the poet has experienced or it may be the poet's interpretative expression of a feeling he or she has gleaned from some other person's experience.

Or the poet may be telling a love story, not necessarily his or her own, Shakespeare's "Romeo and Juliet," for instance.

When Shakespeare gives lines of love to Romeo and/or Juliet, are those lines his? That is, is he revealing his love for Anne Thaxter, maybe, having a character speak his thoughts? Or are Romeo and Juliet's lines simply what Shakespeare would have said were he either character?

In every fiction there is the author's truth. Conversely, in every truth there is fiction, intended or not. Of the latter, we speak or write our "truth" from our perspective. That same "truth" reported by another might be different. That's why it's said that of war, the victor gets to write its history.

Not that love is war, although sometimes it does seem so, especially if the love failed--and in that instance, it's the loser who gets to write the poems of failed love. When love fails, the one who does the jilting or dumping never writes about it; the rejected, jilted lover does.

So, are love poems fact or fiction? Well, some are, some are not, and some are both, embellished by "what if" and "if only" and embroidered dreams and/or nightmares.

Love is a feeling, an emotion, pure and simple, and a poem reflects what is felt.

Is "pure and simple" true? The emotion may be pure but it is not simple. Love can be very complicated, as Romeo and Juliet attest, and love can lead to disaster and destructive ends, again as demonstrated by Romeo and Juliet.

It is the telling that should be simple, bit by bit, or act by act. I saw a production of "Romeo and Juliet" in

Manchester, England, almost forty years ago. It was one of the most memorable theatrical experiences of my life. It wasn't the play, which I had seen before and have seen since; it was that Romeo and Juliet, played with such skill by two young people, became totally real, the only time I have seen that play in which, for me, that happened.

Fiction? Of course. Truth? Yes. I remember that night. At performance end, I cheered the cast, my eyes moist with sadness. Somewhere along the way I had ceased being the audience and had become a part of the play itself,

Since the debate goes on still: who was Shakespeare, was there a Shakespeare, if there was a Shakespeare, did he write the plays? And if he did, was Shakespeare actually there, in Romeo and Juliet's tragic love story? Of course not, but I've thought often that he had to have felt, before he ever wrote them, the lines he gave the doomed hero and heroine.

So it is with any love poem. The poem may not be the poet's report of her or his immediate and/or deeply personal experience, but the poem could never have been written had the poet not had such feelings.

Bear with me while I mention one last thought about Romeo and Juliet. They are young people, fifteen, sixteen, seventeen depending on one's reading of the original folio, adolescents just beginning to emerge into adulthood. Shakespeare goes to great lengths to let us know how young they are, and yet, sometimes, they speak words beyond their youthful experience. It's as if Shakespeare was speaking words from his youth but with the knowledge of an older person. Juliet and Romeo know some of the forces arrayed against their love; they do not know or understand the consequences of their love. That only the older play writer and the audience knows.

The difference is something we know in our senior

lives; we did not take it into account when we were younger. Experience, knowledge, wisdom, if we have learned to use what we have learned, tells us how carefully we have to maintain love, how hard we have to work to enjoy it, how diligent we have to be in sharing it--against all the odds that being seniors throws against us and our partners.

Experiencing the youthful Juliet and Romeo, we are swept away by their love. Their age is important to the play; their love is ageless. Old women and old men know the passion that defies the odds, know the dangers, even may know the potential tragic end, not in death as with Juliet and Romeo but with the death of love itself. And still, aged and wise, we risk everything for the love of a man or a woman.

That we write at all is witness to our continued living. It's easy to write a love poem when your beloved awaits your words and receives them willingly. You are showing your love, expressing it on paper, revealing your heart. For most of us, good poetry or bad, it's not the words but the message of love that counts. Thank goodness for that. Our loved one seeks our message, reassured we mean what we write however faulty the form, because our intent is sure and pure. We can "get away with" a lot of bad poetry as long as we convey the truth of the deep and abiding love that produced it.

Not so with poems of rejection; they're harder to write because, from the poet's point of view, love is tainted with a deep and lasting pain. There's no joy writing about failed love, no wonder and awe in rejection. Not only did love die, the rejected lover cannot help but think of her/himself as a loser with a capital "L." The ego, the inner self, is not only questioned but found wanting.

Further, love can easily turn to hate, and the poet struggles to keep such a negative thought out of the poems lest disappointment and defeat tarnish what once was a priceless gift: someone's love.

In a poem expressing love, one is allowed to exaggerate the truth. Your plain Joe or plain Jane can be gorgeous or beautiful, and is in your eyes. You are encouraged to multiply your loved one's virtues, and you do believe what you see. The love light in your eyes is made to shine brightly, bathing your loved one in a mystic glow of adoration. You might, in your eyes, see someone whose head is crowned with a halo. It's all true--for you.

When you are the rejected lover, the halo disappears and the heavenly glow is darkened. Now your feelings are of despair and defeat; your ego is shattered; your dreams are both denied and smashed. Life has become cruel and pain fills your heart, replacing the ecstasy you experienced before. Now you write, a last cigarette before your execution, a last will and testament for a dead love affair.

You recount your failings, find the heretofore undiscovered premonitions of failure, question this act or that omission; the feelings are dark, and one reason poems of rejection are so difficult to write is that amid the darkness you can find no spark of light. You are not loved--and there is nothing you can do about it.

Except....except reject the bitterness that inevitably comes with rejection. Should the one you loved read your poems of rejection, he/she will find ways to point out your warts, to tell you you were wrong, point out your untruths (from his/her viewpoint), make sure you are the culprit. It comes with the territory. Accept it. You have no choice, of course, but you can choose how you write about your loss. In the midst of pain, report that pain but also report the joy that once was yours, for that joy is as much the truth as is the hurt.

Sunlight and Bright Red Roses

Fall arrived unexpectedly,
inevitably, and 'though
its certain arrival was known,
its swift coming swept away
Summer.
Sudden, chilled airs focused the nerves,
leaves and grasses flashed colors
that like Summer before faded;
the year died, my sense
sadness.
I mourned the time gone by, the tasks
undone, pathways not taken,
sights unseen, love thoughts never shared,
life drained of robust intent.
Listless,
quietly entering Winter,
clothed in regret for brighter
seasons wasted, bemoaning fate,
disappointed with Summer,
denied
Spring colors and Summer flowers,
sunlight and roses, all my
seasons had become Fall, a cruel
dash toward the fearful Winter
until
you revealed the newness of Spring
and the light of Summer suns.
You let me love you, and giving
love in return, you transformed
dark Fall
into Springtime and Summertime
and the unyielding Winter
into a season of light and
laughter and love and bright red
roses.

Cuteness Revisited

"Just sit there and look cute."
How respond to that?
The last time I looked cute
I was three years old and I was looking
at my brand new brother,
wondering what it was
and why would I want one
and how come it smelled.
I must have smiled when the picture was taken,
smiled because if I smelled like that
I'd get a spanking,
and messy brother, you'll get one
and they'll ignore me.
At three I knew a good joke
when I smelled one.

So either sit and look cute
is a throwaway line
or I am about to be the butt of a joke.
Cute I'm not, 'though smarter than three,
and I've figured it out.
Sit and look cute is her way of saying,
"Stay out of my way" or "This is my kitchen"
or "Can't you find something to do?"
Most everything I think is cute
also is pathetically dumb.
Is she suggesting...?

On Nap and Josephine's Love Seat

Oh, how I envied the owner of that love seat,
authenticated Napoleonic antique.
Maybe that's where the emperor and Josephine made love.
Is it a love seat because they made love on it
or because they made love on it it's called a love seat?
I always meant to check that out. And on this very seat?

The piece came to auction. The opening bid far exceeded my
                                                    highest.
"Sold to Number 369."
It's been written up. Not solid wood but veneer,
cheap pine, boxwood, poplar underneath.
The beauty was in the veneer, and when the veneer lifted....

I'd always thought, as with people, after many years
what was underneath became whatever veneer was.
I and number 369 were wrong.
Skip the veneer and find what's underneath,
a true, solid core or, I've learned, scrap wood and worms.

No wonder Napoleon always had his hand in his vest; he was
                                                    scratching.
No wonder Josephine's pictures look as though she's sucking
                                                    lemons.
Perhaps the love seat really wasn't a seat of love at all.
Veneer that hides the truth can make you think that, you know.

So Much for Happiness

"I don't aim for happiness,"
you said in rehearsed words.
"I seek pleasures."
We sipped our liquid pleasure.
Could I fill your glass
with milk and honey?
I wondered why pleasure
outweighed happiness.
In search of Hedon,
you sipped from flasks with him and her.
Pleasure is measured in ounces,
its length in days.
Happiness is an ocean wave
rolling on forever.
I wanted to be that wave,
wasn't even a ripple.
Like the ice that cooled your drink,
I served my purpose and melted away.

Crumbs on the Butter

It was an ultimatum:
slice from the end,
either end, but scrape not from top
or sides. Little
curlicues, cute helixes
or not, forbidden,
a little habit, single
days born, when no one was there
to see or care.
The sternness of her command
killed that habit;
curls of creamy butter died
in fright that day.
On guard. My conscience told me
little habits
become major offenses.
And all was well
until the day I challenged
fate and raised her ire.
Three miniscule crumbs of toast,
each just a speck,
sparkled on creamy butter,
shouting at her.
"See us," they cried, "butter crumbs!"
Crumbs on butter!
No atom bomb exploded
louder; no crime
demanded more punishment.
Crumbs on butter!
She counted not three but four.
Compound the deed
I did. I tried to defend

the little guys
so benign and innocent.
So there were four.
Four! She got close, counted more,
but more than four
was her imagination.
She wiped away
the soiled, offending presence.
"Never," she said,
too angry to continue.
Ultimatum?
Never what? Too scared to ask,
I took dishes
to the sink. Never again?
Never eat toast?
Never dare touch the butter?
Never, ever.
Never, ever be oneself,
always on guard
lest some other dread habit
reveal uncouth
social gracelessness, more proof
that never means
no, end, not a chance. Two are
enough; that's all.
Insult butter, insult me.
Four little crumbs.

An Incident on the Rocky Road

None noticed nor had thought to wonder: there,
one more lost soul on the road to nowhere,
All have been lost to one degree or other,
no pole star to steer our direction right.
Thus it was I joined the trudging many
and took the comfort offered by other waywards.

There was no pity, nor was pity sought.
Lately, the road had become narrow to sight
and tiny pebbles became mountains to climb.
One must be aware: grains of sand turned mount
can prove insurmountable and the summit
beyond seem an unobtainable goal.

I'd heard it happened, witnessed it, in fact,
but never thought to know the truth myself.
Yet there, all of a sudden, my rock strewn path
expanded into a broad, ample road.
What? Why? Who? Standing there, beckoning me
was she, hand outreached, saying, "Follow me."

Oh, Sweet Day!, when North Star came down to
earth,
in earthly form showed the way, provided light.
Oh, Life!, when proffered love turned gravel road
to gold. No mount was high. On dim horizon
rebirthed new Camelots and Avalons,
all promised on my weary road that day.

Oh, Light!, were you too bright for tired eyes?
Blinded by the searing flame of found love,
I stumbled, tripped by an unseen grain of sand.

Was she not real? Did she show herself only
to withdraw, a trick? Perhaps a metaphor:
the light of love exists but not for you?

Mountains are higher now, summits beyond sight.
The path is narrower, more treacherous.
I'm convinced she was real, that for a moment
she chose me. I did see her. And I blinked,
and in the blinking of an eye, she was gone
and I walk the waywards' road lost and alone.

Dancing for Life

Reel, polka, jig, fling,
round, square, slide, and swing,
tap, toe, belly dance,
folk and fancy dance,
improvisation,
interpretation,
one step, two-step, waltz --
life is empty, bare,
in vain, even false,
without the rhythmic flair
of serpentine prints,
marks of rhythm-hints
that catch the measured
beats of life, treasured
primal rhythms felt
where the bluebells bloom
and the moss is soft,
felt from inmost womb
and living undercroft.

Hallelujah, I'm a Bum

It was in tough times when Al Jolson, the leading bum, sang, "Hallelujah, I'm a bum....I'm a bum again," with much bounce and glee.

The song was a recognition of the fact of Depression life, the fall of so many from their burlesque-like social heights, those for whom "the black bottom" and "the camel-walk" were dances, who first called women's breasts "boobs," when society girls were called "bright young things," when "boogie-woogie" was a party and "Gibsons" and "gimlets" and "sidecars" were the newest faddish drinks, when everything nice was "the cat's whiskers," when society women had their corgis and other can't-go-without lap dogs, when the word "debunk" entered the English language, and when Jolson pricked the pretentious bubbles of the used-to-be rich who had fought so failingly to avoid financial disaster and who, finally, accepted that they, too, were bums.

Bums were, well, almost every man and woman; bums were no longer alone at the bottom of the social ladder; they had plenty of company; almost everyone was at the bottom.

Those who had been there from the first knew how to be a bum; all the others didn't.

When Jolson sang the Rodgers and Hart song, he gave bums and being a bum a meaning Americans of the Depression could understand: recognizing what you are gives you the freedom to be what you are.

Being a bum isn't being much, but knowing you're a bum and accepting that condition allows you to enjoy what life grants you. If you didn't want to be a bum, didn't want to be a loser, you struggled against bumship; you wouldn't be victorious for long; now you're a bum again. Hallelujah! It was classic stoicism at its best.

Well, the situation is similar when a new love fails you. You love, so high on the emotional ladder. You have all the riches love can supply. Then love crashes and you feel as though you've fallen into a dark, bottomless pit. You are lost and you are a loser. You hate it; you moan and cry and rail against the gods and the Fates. You call yourself all kinds of names. You beg; no one pays any attention. They call you "Big L."

You're not alone, but you think you are. You're at life's bottom, and there you stay. If you're lucky, you realize you're not the only one who's been there; you do have soulmates, miserable as they are.

And if you're very lucky (or have become very wise), you'll look up from the bottom of your pit and see daylight. You won't see the beaming face of the one you loved; he/she will not be there with outstretched arms offering you salvation. Actually, your chances are better that you'll see his/her boot ready to stomp you down.

But you'll climb, and as you climb, recrimination and depression and defeat are left behind. It will take time; you will give it time because your whole future life either will remain in that hole of despair or will be found somewhere in the sunlight above.

You'll reach the top. And in the sunlight you'll sing, "Hallelujah, free again." His/her image will be there; you will not forget it, but no longer will he/she reduce you to pitiful playdough. "Hallelujah, I'm a free person again." You'll rejoin the living, wiser maybe, at least wise enough to know you were not just one of those for whom love failed, wise enough to know it was not love that failed, only your love for that special someone.

Now you're free. The bond that became a hangman's

noose has been severed. The memories that choked you remain, but no longer do they strangle you, breathtaking fetters that stilled the dream.

All that has been let go. You're free to live in the light again. Hallelujah!

Between the Stars

Once, I saw the heavens;
a trillion great bright stars
appeared and winked at me.
Now, when I dare look up,
I see black space between,
and heaven fades from view.
I never feared the dark
until now. Twilight is,
and forever dark is near.
The stars have left the sky,
taking everything dear.

First the Light and then....

Unguarded, I let you pass
through the gateway of my eyes;
     you entered my heart,
     took residence there,
     and from there my soul.
Life was pure, the finest gold;
life burned, a ruby red flame;
     natural, perfect,
     each day round, white pearls;
     flawless, diamond bright.
I found you so and spoke it,
you who dispelled the old fears
     and banished nightmares
     with light and beauty,
     with "I love you" words.

     Now, what truth to tell?
     Momentary game?
     Charade? No "right stuff?"
The heart lies broken, shattered,
the soul lost and bewildered.
     Fool's gold is tarnished;
     ruby red is blood
     spilled from fractured heart;
pearls dissolve in tears; diamond
light reflects only darkness.
     What would I speak now?
     The light has gone out
     and with it beauty.
You turned your back and denied
my heart and soul. Why, Love, why?

Ice Ages

I

Stark, silent, unmoving,
the turned back screams negation
and in the gloom provides
its own exclamation point,
a message without words
mimed in practiced rigid pose.
A giant icicle,
the point honed and polished in
encore performances,
with lethal intent or not,
is thrust toward oft made wounds
and leaves no outward mark.

II

Sheets of snow go on forever
and in nearly dark appear to glow,
reflections of longleaf crystals,
new laid frost atop the snow.
A single mound of drifted fluff
deflects an infinite view.
Cast loose in sterile frigid waste,
there's but frustration to subdue.

III

Icicles were childhood pleasure,
swords, ball bats, little darts,
from maple trees bitter-tasty,
charms of crystals, winter's arts.
When they grew, we knew long winter;

when they dripped, spring was near.
Icicles, what we could make of them,
reflected the atmosphere.
Who would have guessed tapering spikes
would chill our later years,
that now grow long, cold icicles
and hope for warmth disappears.

IV

No
is cold
without hope,
leaves no room for
anticipation
and steals away the dream.
Rejected hearts give up,
not all at once, but
in the frigid atmosphere,
they grow
cold.
Not
able
to create
sustaining warmth
enough to maintain
hope in shivering cold,
they too become frigid
and reflect the ice-
house images
of their re-
jected
selves.

Her Hourglass

Crystal precious,
small hourglass
telling no time
but from a time
of memory
(A lover's gift
before my time?)
in transit lost.

Making time mine,
I bought its mate.
No sooner done,
original
then reappeared.
Arresting pair:
before and now.

One disappeared,
the one before
or mine? Who knew?
Replaced again,
the hourglass
revealed now time:
did I return
what I had snitched?

Once I had meant
love timelessly;
now drifts time sands
through sandless glass,
love, affection
substituted
with doubt, mistrust.

Reflected in a Movie Theme

You came having given love
elsewhere
and before.
I claimed only what was mine
and found it wasn't
mine alone
or even mine at all.
For all I knew
it never was,
just as you said
it wasn't
and never would be,
and it wasn't,
but it was there
for someone else
at times.
I shouldn't claim what wasn't mine,
but I did,
pretending not to know
but knowing all along
that what I claimed
had been claimed
before my time
and during.
To be opened only by those
with a need to know.
More than you knew,
I knew, and I couldn't claim what
wasn't mine
and didn't.
And when I didn't,
you never asked why.

Her Motto: Not Forgiveness, Revenge

Oh, Nemesis, Nox's harsh daughter,
Divine Vengeance,
who leads the virtueless to slaughter,
you who sentence
hapless mortals to black misery,
what fault did I
possess or crime against thee commit?
Through Walton's eye:
     "And though circuitous and obscure
     The face of Nemesis how sure!"
For what impiety found you fault
that you visit
me with loss and suffering and assault
this simple twit
whose only sin, perhaps, too much love?
Ah, Nemesis,
though you hide behind another name,
Greek Rhamnusis,
Adrastia, Rhumnusia,
it is the same.
Nor hide thee behind your given name,
bound forever
to a saint's pure, gentle tenderness,
not whatever
you became, filled with vengefulness.
Oh, Greek goddess,
you who can measure out happiness
as well as stress,
"she whom no man may escape," set free
your victim. Oh,
lift the punishment pronounced on me,
soft light bestow.

Me Jane; You Tarzan

It was simple enough. Even romantic. Two people lost in life's jungle discover one another and live together happily ever after. I never did understand why Jane and Tarzan spoke a kind of pidgin English, but that's a different matter entirely.

When Edgar Rice Burroughs introduced us to Tarzan of the Apes (1914), and later when Johnny Weissmuller appeared in the first Tarzan film (1932), we had a new metaphorical image of the male/female thing. Besides swashbuckling swordsmen and gun totting defenders of cattle and women, in that order, we had a man and a woman battling nature itself. Never mind that early Tarzan movies were shot on the Cornell University campus, in the wilds of primitive Africa a man and, later, a woman struggled against nature in the guise of the jungle, elevating the human struggle to cosmic heights not popularized since the Greek dramatists twenty centuries before.

The risk of oversimplification is great; I don't want to run that risk. Tarzan and Jane are dime novel characters, Tarzan a super man figure, Jane a super wife (mate, really, nothing more) and a super mom when Boy came along. Together they fought bad African natives, bad Nordic-type whites, bad jungle creatures. They prevailed against fang and claw, against spears and arrows, against guns.

Consider the earliest Tarzan adventures. He struggled against the jungle. "Against" is the operative word. He was a long time learning to be part of it--and when he did, he was saved from himself, his isolation, his loneliness, his permanent fear.

In a way, humans still are learning Tarzan's lessons, that it's not man/woman against nature but man/woman cooperating with nature. That was the very first lesson, if lesson is the correct word, that Burroughs provided.

However, as important as is cooperation with our world rather than the Biblical "have dominion over," that's not why I direct your attention to Tarzan and Jane. Rather, most of us are alone and incomplete until we meet our Tarzan, our Jane, the one, in Burroughs' imaginative figures, who comes out of nowhere to be our partner.

Not that you and I at our ages are going to swing from trees, call elephants and lions to our aid, make pals with monkeys (okay, maybe we will do that or have friends who will make monkeys of us). We will, with our Tarzan or Jane, feel a power and a strength and a purpose we didn't know we had or thought we had lost.

I can say without fear of contradiction, if you and I go about swinging from trees, we're either a mental case or headed for the emergency ward--or both.

Yet in our minds, we could--or we would if necessary--to prove our love. If someone asks you to swing on the honeysuckle or wisteria vines, he/she has a death wish. Yours. The same if you're asked to step into the wild felines' cage at the local zoo. Don't! And I doubt you want for your best friend an ape or a monkey (but at least you won't have to buy him/her a fur coat.)

When I was a youngster, my mother and brother and I spent our winter months in a city outside of Boston. The bank owned apartments were filled with Depression children. Play was what we made up for ourselves, and for the boys, part of our play was in a Reservation four or five miles from home. There was an old stone sheepfold and a stone tower, but what directed our attention was a cave, a panther's cave (so we believed), the result of the last ice age, high up on a granite cliff. One got to the cave by sliding down an old tree. It must have been a popular spot because the tree trunk was as smooth as glass. Nobody ever was able to shinny back up. Down to the bottom of a valley was via another old tree just as smooth. We were all Tarzan. We did whatever Tarzan did in the latest story. The wonder was nobody ever got hurt, even when someone found rope and we swung wildly off into space and onto other trees.

I guess we were too young to give serious thought to Jane. We didn't play cowboys and Indians, just Tarzan. Our bicycles, those who had them, were lions and tigers, and we rode double, Tarzan and Tarzan. We treated our forest playground with respect, never left papers or evidence of our passing. It was a secret place, and secrets had to be kept secret.

What I remember is that getting to the cave took some courage; getting out and down from the cave took more courage. Some of us never would have managed alone; we needed the companionship and encouragement of another, and behind it all was our image of brave, resourceful, strong Tarzan, King of the Jungle.

As with my brother and me, many of our friends were without fathers. We had no male model in the home. For all the boys present, it was a female world, and thus Tarzan became, albeit unconsciously, a role model. I can't say why Tarzan and not someone else; it just happened.

In a far away world none of us could imagine, suffering depravations all of us could imagine, for a couple of years Tarzan was our hero, and we acted out his adventures in our forest playground.

Much was fantasy. Other than skunks and snakes, we met few wild animals, not counting the mice and rats that inhabited the neighborhood. We escaped our troubles by imagining new and different ones, troubles we could overcome with cunning and strength, unlike the Depression reality we faced.

There were far fewer girls than boys in our neighborhood, a sociological quirk of circumstantial biology, to coin a phrase, and I have no idea what the girls did similarly, if there was a similarity, to boys' play.

But this I remember, because years later friends would comment on it: we wanted to be heroic, to rise above our world, to take on the perils of life and emerge victorious. That was ancient history, but even now, even in old age, men want to be seen as strong and vibrant and resourceful, to have Jane say, no matter her name, "I Jane; you Tarzan," and mean it.

Janes and Tarzans do not come into our lives more than once or twice, if we are lucky. To be someone's hero or heroine, however frail we may be, is to refind life.

Tarzan and Jane are any couple confronting their jungle, green or asphalt, struggling against all kinds of adversities. Because of their union, they will prevail. That's Burroughs' ultimate message. And almost a hundred years later, it is the defining message of the strength of love: two are stronger than ten or a hundred; two can overcome all trials life sets before them; two can conquer their world and live happily ever after.

Homecoming

I was nobody;
you made me somebody.
I drifted without aim;
you gave me direction.
I was one of the lost;
you found me and you said,
welcome home; here is life.
I was lifeless and into me
you breathed your spirit.

Give Me Your Breath

Indian legend has it
that sometimes a man's breath is
taken away, hidden, and
he can't live long without it.
Some say spirits, good, evil,
do that to an Indian
who will spend the rest of life
looking for his hidden breath.

I thought that another myth
until you appeared and stole
my breath away and hid it
I know not where. You, spirit,
are you good or evil? Will
you restore my breath? Must I
search forever? Or will you
breathe into me your power,
your sweet breath making me strong.

Do Not Open Unless Absolutely Necessary

Consider yourself warned. Yes, love does fail, and one way to work through the hurt is to write about it. Already you've read hints of failed love; now you can view the remains so sadly put to rest. Love is beautiful; the rejected lover is not so pretty, and there's no way to fancy dress the pathetic figure who has been defeated and stripped of hope.

There are many ways to jilt a lover. Taking another is clear enough; demanding more than can be given also works in time, as does a deluge of negative, hurtful criticism. Often the jilter delivers blow after blow and the jiltee just doesn't get it, taking the slams and the demeaning kicks, always harboring the forlorn hope that none of it is true or meant for her/him.

Many people don't know how to love; more precisely, how to expand their egos to include another. Some of those same people don't know how to unlove, be there such a word. They know only the way to hurt, taking seeming delight in fang and claw, leaving the former lover bruised and brainless.

Until someone writes a guide on how not to love, painful broken hearts will clutter the streets. They're there, all ages and both genders, in all sizes and shapes, high statused and low casted: losers, double L, lousy losers. For such poor souls William Boyd wrote, "Divinity is only seen in glimpses / and flowers fall off in bloom."

For a time he or she was your morning and evening star, heaven tied, or so it seemed. You possessed life's richest gifts, someone to love and someone who loved you. It was divine, holy even. Out of all this world, from troubles and loss, two souls met and joined hands and hearts and shared rose buds and sunlight and starlight, and beauty was discovered in everything.

Alas, the roses faded and the light dimmed. Dreams became nightmares, hope vanished, promises turned to lies, love was withdrawn and in its place blame and cause. You failed. Whatever it was, you failed. It's no good asking what or why; you might as well ask the stars or the gods or the Fates.

Love can be like that, a sudden burst of bright star-like vitality, and just as suddenly it's gone from the sky, its only trace ashes and your bewildered memory of its momentary luminous radiance. It's no help to say that's part of life, but of course it is, just as love was.

To the religious, the absence of a god's love is hell. Theology aside, when love is withdrawn or lost or denied, we are in a state of gracelessness. Life and a reason for living has been sucked out of us. We have been consigned to a pit of endless emotional torture, and none there hear our cries. Life has become our personal hell.

If you can call it such, there is one redeeming fact in this: there is no way we can be hurt further or suffer more. Small comfort, you say? No comfort is intended, only the admonition to cherish every spark of love while you have it and the hope that when receiving love you will give love in return in far greater measure.

I warned you: you wouldn't like this part. If you're here, I can but wish you'll walk out of your dark stormy weather into a new light. The sun still shines; find where.

A Trigraph Haiku

Frigid winter winds,
much warmer than ice voices
which speak without care.

Nothing blows colder
than demeaning loveless voice.
There is no warmth there.

Such ice chills the soul.
The soul has no cloak against
one who does not care.

Pluperfect

Just one
dozen,
only the fairest chosen from the fair
and sent
with love.
Roses,
her favorite flower, nature's finest,
like her,
beauty.
Thank you.
She saw the beauty and denied the love.
Neither
lasted.

Geography

Wandering, seeking surcress,
pain is everywhere.
Go there, pain is;
stay here, pain is.
Pain's geography.
Joy is where you are.
You are not here.
You were not there either;
I've been there.
You left before I arrived;
only pain was there
because you left
without me;
greater pain
because you knew I was coming.

Mission Accomplished

"Your mission," she'd say,
"if you care to accept it, is...,"
and she'd set out a task.
Always, I accepted, happily
engaged to please her.
Then one day, "Your mission...
is to die." Say What?
"Now, ended. Go away."

Dying isn't hard to do;
it's the dying part, not death
itself; the road to death
is the soul searing part.
Ended. Tossed on the heap.
"Now I lay me down to sleep."
"Your mission, like it or not,
is to accept the naught.
I've love to give but not
to you." Oh, to die like this.
Mission accepted.

One last mission just for you.
I'll go where death is,
just for you, but I will not die.
We're agreed on my demise;
there is no choice; the dead
cannot embrace the living.
I wonder, though, if my mission
was what you really meant,
not death but just to fade away,
go where the others have gone.

The Last Promise

You filled the void
between life and emptiness,
you whom I love
even now in silent ways,
for silence is
your demand. I'll honor that
and silent be
from afar; your request, too.
I do love you
nonetheless. Speak ill of me
as will you must,
poor loser and all the rest,
yet deny not
the truth you know in your heart:
if you had let me,
I would have been good for you.

All Willows Weeping

Beneath their sweeping arms
I let them cry with me.
All willows weeping,
silent chorus, pity.
What does the willow know
'cept the child hid here
in time of fright and fear.
Now the man in misery.
The willows share the tears,
let droplets fall, and leaves,
and hide me in their lea.

Sonnet

Perhaps because you'd flown so far and high
you choose to come to earth, mingle a while
with those who reach for the untouched sky.
Perhaps you came simply to offer a smile,
gay laughter, encouragement, wish us well.
When you didn't leave, when you spoke my name,
when you wrapped me within your goddess spell,
I knew my life never would be the same.
You made me fly and touch the blazing sun,
and when I was burned, you pipped little laughs.
"Now you know," you said, "each star's a blinding
                                             sun
too hot for you," adding di and trigraphs.
I had sought to rope a grand unicorn,
me, a lowly, earthbound, worthless greenhorn.

I Promised You a Rose Garden

Never again
        shall I see a rose
and not think of you.
We never did
        each other good
or plant a garden.

The red rose died,
        and bouquets of roses,
and red flowed,
dried, and turned brown,
        nor pressed to remember.
What's to remember?

Would forget-me-nots
        grow instead?
Grow there, In fallow sand
under desert air?
        Roses don't grow
in dust bowls

watered only by neglect.
        We did each
no good, and where garden
might, weeds and briar thorns
        grow and
bittersweet remains.

On Cleaving

"There's nothing between us" can be taken two ways. The first implies distance, separation if once there was closeness.

The second is a togetherness so close nothing can come between the two people involved. In both a physical sense and an emotional sense, the two cleave, to use an old word.

The injunction, "Let nothing come between you," is offered often as spiritual advice. It is good advice, but it is almost a casual throwaway line if those receiving it do not commit to the hard work implied.

I was told once, "Everybody knows how to love." The evidence, of course, is to the contrary; divorce statistics alone provide doubt. Everybody does not know how to love.

Or if that statement is too radical, then everybody does not know how to make love work--in their favor and in their partner's favor. Love is incomplete without the work and commitment necessary to make it a continuing reality.

The beauty of love is not <u>what</u> brings two people together but what <u>keeps</u> them together.

Oh, don't think I'm dismissing the wonder of the physical and emotional or spiritual awareness of someone and the revelation of your possible future happiness when discovering someone to love and when that love is returned. Try as we do, no one has ever verbally captured the full depth of the romantic feelings, breathless as they are, of being in love. It is indescribably delicious; one is tasting life in its fullest, most robust, utterly sublime presence.

To maintain that realm of euphoria, to have the taste

linger, to move from the first joyous encounter into a future with that person, a future which transforms pleasure into realized happiness, seldom just happens.

Happiness in love is achieved; it is not guaranteed that two people who fall in love will be happy. Quite the contrary; they may end up miserable.

Achieve happiness: the very word "achieve" implies work, effort, trying. Falling in love often is inexplicable magic, wonder, awe.

Staying in love is even more magical, more wonderous, of greater awe because far fewer people stay in love than fall in love.

The magic, wonder and awe of staying in love is different from the mysterious falling in love. Staying, each partner becomes the magician. When lead appears, it is turned into gold. When dark clouds of doubt appear, they are turned into silver clouds of faith and trust. When disagreements arise, as they are certain to do, shared solutions are found.

When love lasts, two people have decided nothing will be allowed to come between them, no argument will remain unsettled, there will be no winner, no loser.

When two people cleave, they come together consciously and with the pledge that their union, their togetherness, their oneness is more important than anything which might separate them.

It is the ultimate pledge one makes to another, and to honor and to fulfill that pledge takes effort.

Many cannot or will not make that effort. For them, love simply was not strong enough, or was not worth enough to be worked at, or never moved from the initial physical and/or emotional attraction to a level of permanence, or was a transitory and temporary fling, a diversion of momentary excitement.

However, if a love is worth keeping, if another person is worth holding on to, if one's future is best entered with that person, if another person is your best friend and is the faithful lover to whom you give your love and fidelity--then make love work.

Making love work is using the vocabulary of love, "we," "us," and "our," not "you" and "me." It is saying "I love you" daily, hourly if necessary, in words that are clear and without condition. It is the touch, the kiss, the physical expression of emotional bonding that is more than carnal urgings. It is wanting to understand when you don't understand. It is patience and tolerance. It is forgiveness and seeking forgiveness. It is inclusion and yet it is the desire for individual growth supported by faith in the other. It is shared household chores, divisions of labor mutually agreed. It is the day to day effort to please. It is the intent to be worthy in the other's sight. It is the granting of freedom to the other to be what he/she struggles to be, and the giving of encouragement and support so that the other grows. It is sharing, even if vicariously, the other's successes and helping the other to succeed. It is correcting one's annoying habits, like leaving crumbs on the butter. It is openness and criticism without rancor or the intent to hurt. It is accepting mention of one's faults or failings without being threatened, and then correcting them.

Working at love is a million things. It is trial and error. Love is meeting trials head on, lessening the errors with your partner by your side, with you by his/her side. Love is sharing the agonies of life together; love is achieving victory together. A true lover is a helpmate and a comforter and a soulmate who with you bears all burdens and shares all sorrows. A true lover is a defender of your honor, your person, your heart. A true lover is there, through thick and thin, bearing your pains and reflecting in your glories.

Yes, love is hard work, yet if you are in love, you aren't aware of the efforts you make, consciously or unconsciously; you are aware only of the priceless, heavenly, divine reward of having someone love you. You are lifted from up out of the sometimes hostile world into a world of bliss.

And if you have worked at love, at loving someone with your whole heart and mind, you are blessed. You and your loved one will have created a world which never can overcome you. You have each other. From each is received love; to each is love given.

Cleaving, nothing can come between you and your loved one; cleaving, you and he/she take on the world; cleaving, nothing can defeat you. The strength of two in love is unlimited--if they work at it.

In Love There is Freedom

Among love's truths, this:

when you love and are loved,
you are free.
Love lifts you above bleak clouds,
moves you beyond yourself,
unites you with heaven.
In a spiritless city, it gives you hope;
in a lonely country, it gives you a companion;
in a dark room, it gives you light;
in the arms of your lover, you are free of doubt
and despair and fear.
You are not poor of wealth, you are rich;
you are not a weak single link,
you are the strength of two;
you are not alone, you are a pair --
and you are free to go wherever destiny leads.
You are freed from the past;
you are free to pursue the future;
you are released from youthful indecision,
unfettered by middle age convention,
the only infirmity the limits of your dreams.
And you are free to dream;
love grants you that freedom.
Nothing else can.

Lyrics: Dream of Me Tonight

Dream of me tonight, / sweet dreams, dear.
Let our love dreams fill / your night.
Close your eyes, my kiss / on your cheek.
Hold your pillow tight, / hug me,
dream of me, my love, / dream of me;
hold me in your dreams.

In the lonesome night, / I dream, too,
and though we're apart, / my heart
holds you near, wishing / dreams came true
and you were near, here / with me.
Let our night dreams touch, heart to heart;
Love with love's dreaming.

Life's Blessing

Blessed is the woman
who can say, "I've found
my Adam" or the man
who joyfully claims,
"Yes, I have my Eve."
Love gives; love receives.
Love supports, sustains,
encourages. Love
understands failure,
builds hope, fulfills dreams.
No trial is too hard,
no wasteland too vast
when from genesis
two hearts beat as one.
Love holds and comforts.
Love is life's blessing.

Myth and Reality: An Afterword

Actually, it's several words.

The Greeks of old told of a man and of a man's long journey to reach home and love. The man was Odysseus and because of his name, a long, difficult journey has been called an odyssey.

Odysseus had been separated from all he knew and loved for a long time. On his way home from the Trojan wars, he met the goddess Calypso, and she, pleased by Odysseus, promises to make him a god, beautiful, immortal, ageless, his infinite life carefree and unmarred.

Odysseus was tempted. Who wouldn't be? He'd fought his battles; he'd been alone for so long. Now there was someone who wanted him and who offered a land of milk and honey and beauty and an eternity free of struggle and strife and the pain of solitude.

Odysseus turned all that down: the days of drinking the juice of the grape, the romantic nights, the opportunity to avoid aging and death, imperfection and the continued risks of his voyage into and for an uncertain future.

Why? Why not be a god? Wouldn't we all be gods, and goddesses, if we could? Who would refuse a life with Calypso were it offered? Or with Odysseus were he a god?

Perhaps we have been separated from someone to love, have been on our own odyssey, have faced tough times, have been alone.

And then there is someone, if not Calypso someone divine and beautiful or handsome, who promises an eternity of love and beauty. What's wrong with that picture? On our own pleasure island?

Odysseus knew. He refused an everlasting life of

youthfulness and tranquility with a goddess, and rejected becoming a god, because heroism in life is something to which the gods cannot aspire. There would be no life, not in the human sense. Toward what would one work, why would one need to have courage or integrity, in whom could one believe and have faith, how could one achieve love or join with someone in sharing or from whom would one received comfort and support--all meaningless virtues because they are not needed by the gods?

Odysseus turned Calypso down, choosing Penelope, she of the aging body, mortal, flawed and frail, a human woman. Odysseus's and Calypso's lovemaking is pleasant; Odysseus's and Penelope's lovemaking is passionate.

What makes the difference? Needing no one, gods and goddesses are without an adventurous spirit. Having all pleasures, they do not seek happiness. They have no need to exchange love words; they take no risks; they savor no victories; they share no ideas; they do not offer support because they need none; they are self-centered because they are gods and goddesses. Calypso, like all the old Greek gods and goddesses (and Roman and many others), had, from Odysseus's human point of view, one flaw: they were perfect and knew it, and knowing their perfection, they were selfish.

That's what Odysseus knew. You can't love a god or goddess; he or she doesn't need you. Calypso didn't need Odysseus, only that he provided her with pleasure. She didn't, couldn't, love him. If she loved, it was only herself.

It takes two mortal people to know love. Penelope, the human woman, did love Odysseus. She did not know Odysseus's whole story, so she listened. He did not know the whole of her story, so she told it, and Odysseus listened. Sharing their trials and pains, sharing their hopes and dreams, they confronted, as imperfect as they were, the risks of their mortality, knowing their certain finite lives but choosing to live them together, daringly, passionately, loving each other as only humans can.

Calypso, "that goddess most divinely made," was perfect; Penelope was, well, an imperfect human woman; Odysseus was not the perfect man. He, too, was aging, growing frail, burdened with human flaws. Such are the facts when one's not an immortal deity.

In a way, we each are confronted with Odysseus's choice: find a god or goddess with whom to have pleasure-- or discover one who is human with whom to share love. In Homer's epic, we cannot become truly human until we love and accept another's love.

It's all a myth or a legend, you'll say. Perhaps.

> My lady goddess, here is no cause for anger.
> My quiet Penelope--how well I know--
> would seem a shade before your majesty,
> death and old age being unknown to you,
> while she must die. ...
> ... Let the trial come.
> Robert Fitzgerald translation

Trial? The trial of finding Penelope--and the trial of living a mortal's life.

No matter how old we are, although when we were young we were not aware of it--only with age does it become apparent, we live our lives precariously balanced on a metaphorical razor's edge. On one side of us is reality and on the other side is what some call mythos, that is, dreams (images) and wishes. Perhaps Calypso or her opposite gender counterpart was only that.

Our balancing between mythos and reality is no high wire circus act; the skill needed is not so much the balancing as it is keeping in touch with what is on either side of our perilous edge, what is real (reality) on one side and what we hope will become real on the other (dreams, image, mythos).

Calypso is not the human Odysseus's reality, Penelope is. Just as life for Adam and Eve in Eden was sterile and essentially meaningless, without adventure and the sense of accomplishment, pleasant but not happy, so life with Calypso would be without meaning and purpose. Wise men and women do not seek such dream worlds; they make their own worlds with their Penelope or their Odysseus.

Our years of experience have taught us that too big a dose of reality can lead to spiritless cynicism and that too many wild dreams and groundless hopes can be an excursion into a land of wild fantasy and hallucination.

Granted, life on the razor's edge can become a kind of reality, and perching there can become a kind of pseudo-existence. Positioned uncomfortably midway between reality and mythos, as was Odysseus for a time, one neither ascends nor descends; one clings, and clinging to maintain our balance can become the one and only purpose of life. When that is so, the razor's edge itself may appear to be the sum of all things and events. It's not so.

It's not so because there is no security on the razor's edge; to exist there is painful; to exist there is contrary to one's knowledge and consciousness; to exist there is to know only doubt and fear along with the pain.

We know that on one side there are greater realities; we know on the other side are potential new themes and plots for our lives. The trick is to reach for the truths and insights and rewards on both sides without falling off completely to either side.

The emotionally healthy person is not merely straddling, which brings its own severe discomfort, but rather is reaching toward the side of existent things while at the same time reaching toward his/her hopes and dreams. At our best, it's a simultaneous act.

And that's what Odysseus did. He rejected the god's life for his life with Penelope--and both he and she struggled to create in their finite lives and time their own land of beauty in which love was both their security and their reason for venturing into the future.

The point is, on one side we think rationally and analytically, on the other side we think emotionally and poetically. There is truth on both sides, and when we reach for and achieve insights from both, we blunt the razor edge on which we sit and from there create new meanings for our lives.

To use the ancient prophet's, Ezekiel's, idea:

> There is a time for reason;
> there is a time for emotion.
> There is a season for speaking prose;
> there is a season for poetry.
> There is an occasion for rational analysis;
> there is an occasion for creative imagination.

The danger of total reality without dreams and fictional images is its accompanying sense of depression, hopelessness and defeat. Much of Odysseus's sojourn was just that. The risk of living only in wishful thinking and myth, as with Calypso, was its unconnectedness, remoteness and basic untruthfulness.

You would be correct to point out that without plenty of reality there would be no sciences, no medicines, and that without dreams and aspirations there would be no art or music. And you would be correct to point out that without imagination, there would be no discoveries, and that without images of what might be, there would be no inventions, no literature, no singing, not even, perhaps, future realities.

Because in fantasy and in our dreams there is love; in reality there is no harmony, perhaps only discord; in reality there is conflict; in mythos there is peace. Specifically, with senior love, reality is what is; mythos is what might be. So there we are on our razor's edge wondering if we should or could love again at our age and if there might be someone who could and would love us.

Reality demands a search, a quest, if you will, Odysseus's journey; imagination projects a discovery, even a rescue, not by Calypso but by Penelope. When the imagined "might be" is realized, a new reality is created, existence is enhanced, the razor's edge becomes a solid, secure platform, and there Odysseus and Penelope dwelt.

Those who dare dream go beyond their present reality. Myth reflects in metaphorical images the real and transcends the real, projecting future realities.

Is there a risk? Of course, a great risk that our realities will defeat our grand illusions. But what is worse, spending one's remaining life balancing or taking one's life in hand and reaching out and up, even if the reaching ends in failure?

You decide, as of course you will. I would suggest that to give up before you have tried is self-defeating, is falling off into reality so completely that only sour and dreadful consequences are certain.

The poems you have just read are love poems, both reaching and reality lines. In the lines, love sometimes is used as a noun (my love) or a verb (I love you) or an adjective (love poem). Love is something we feel and something we do. It also is a score in tennis, meaning zero, zilch, naught. I've mentioned that, too, because the concept of zero is just as much a reality as is a million. To score love in love is the risk, the reality born of failed mythos.

But not to dream? Since all of this is about seniors and senior love, perhaps it's proper to close with two lines from George Bernard Shaw's play, "Back to Methuselah," Mr. M being the oldest of the old: "You see things and you say, 'Why?' But I dream things that never were, and I say, 'Why Not?'"

Why--why bother, why try, why care?--is being beaten down by too much reality. Why not--why not try, why not plan, why not love?--is allowing the "might be" to have its chance.

"Get real" sometimes means to stop trying, that what you dream is an impossible dream, that "might be" never will be. If you "get real" in that sense, you'll never know what's possible; you'll exist paralyzed on your razor's edge, unable to move. Existence is not the human essence. "I dream things that never were, and say, 'Why not?'" Why not, indeed. That's the essence of our lives that keeps us young and hopeful and able to love and respond to love. Why not? Go for it! Dream. But dream not to avoid or retreat from reality but to run forward into the future. No risk should be too great, no "why" should stop you. Yell "Why not!" and charge hell-bent-for-leather into the sunset. Chance that your myth will become your reality from which even more wondrous images will flow.

The last poem in this book is written with no punctuation; sentences are open ended by my choice, not by a typesetter's mistake. The reason is simple. Periods mean something has come to an end. Like all these sentences. But love knows no end nor is it limited by grammatical boundaries. The lack of end punctuation symbolizes more, more than the words can express, more to come: more love, more adventures, more life. As seniors, we have been on a long journey, much of it when we took first steps into the unknown future. There still is an unknown future before us;

our journey is incomplete. We have not stamped a period at the end of our lives; our lives are open ended, and if we share them with someone, we can and will step into the new future with brave and confident hearts.

When the bloom of youth has passed, when the brow sweats from the ardors of trials, when the body loses its strength, when wrinkles appear, when the eyes dim, the hair thins, the flesh begins to sag--all those things that come upon us with the years--how grand to hold the hand of the one we love and to face the sunrise of each new day with the courage born of two hearts. It does happen. Passion knows no age. Expressed differently, perhaps, caring, sharing, daring the risks are ageless. As mortal and infinite as we are, to love someone is eternally pure; to be loved by someone is to be sublimely victorious in a world of our making. Nothing, not age or weakness or even death, can take from us the splendor of a loving man or a loving woman.

Lyrics: Sometimes When You Touch Me

Sometimes when you touch me
and it's late at night,
when you touch me,
my heart takes to flight.
Sometimes when you hold me,
my heart is made still;
I can't believe
you love me tonight.

And then when you kiss me,
all my dreams come true.
In dark of night,
all my worries rest:
you make everything right.
Loving at this time
is best; being loved
by you, I'm blesssed.

In A Tourist Town on a Summer Day

Amid the many, alone,
nor does one seek to atone
for separateness among
the many. The crowded streets,
shops, highway, byway traffic,
strangers most, tucked in attic
or closet thoughts, too many
seen but unknown, we and them,
among whom we don't exist,
nor they. Yet the seen persist
and to them we are the seen,
the same unknown and not seen.
Why then, just why do I long
to be like them, to belong
to someone, to walk the streets
hand in hand, to shop the aisles,
to sit in auto lines, crowds,
too many people, smog clouds
choking air and pristine view?
What is there within the hordes
that draws me from separateness?
Not the many, herd-like mess,
pressing, bumping and careless,
tourist and native stampedes.

Not the crowds. Amid the crowd
people, moments, light allowed.
There, she holds his arm and points,
and for a moment they share
a private delight. And there,
he leads her down an aisle where

lies a gourmet treasure. See,
he says, over to the right,
picture the flowered archway;
the beauty has made our day.
That's it; it's all so simple:
the many mean nothing till
among the many is seen
the meaningful human scene,
individuality -
the one who is of the crowd -
and pairs. Ah, it's the pairing
that belies alone, sharing
sights and chores, finding pleasure
in first seen vistas, being
together in adventure,
each moment holy and pure.
Such sights create a longing.
To someone I would belong.

My Hollyhock

Blown in on a fortuitous wind,
    carried by birds or uninvited furred guests,
how proudly it stands,
    and how lonely,
struggling for life in a concrete crack.

I'd transplant you, I tell it,
    if I could,
but how get to the root of you
      buried in hardened slurry?

I should plant a mate,
but that would be my choosing,
      not his. Or is it a she? Or Both?
      Or neither.
What are hollyhocks anyway?

You belong in the garden, I tell it,
    not here;
there is no life here,
      only harshness and cruel grains of sand.
      They were a majestic mountain;
      once they overlooked the endless horizon;
         dreams like pure spindrift
         rolled from their summits.

Ah, you know. You're reaching for them
    somewhere toward the sun.

I understand you, lost in your concrete shoes.
I'll guard you. We have much in common
    for I, too, fell between the cracks,
    my blossoms shorn before full bloom.

Too Much for One Heart to Hold

Too much
        too much joy, too much happiness, too much beauty
        for one heart to hold
Close to bursting
        I will explode, I fear. I can't contain it all
I can't even comprehend what you've done
        beyond thought
        beyond and deeper
down to where primal and primitive life begins
        beyond into dreams
        beyond the stars
deeper and higher in breathless heart beats
        deeper than the ocean plunges to deep
        higher than any telescope can reach
How can my heart hold you in

Such words
        too simple. They don't begin to explain
They don't do justice
        to what you mean
        No vocabulary of love could
That's the truth
        I don't have the words
Thoughts of you outrace the words
        thus the simplest must be profound
You're more than the world to me
You're my universe,
        my sun, my moon, my stars,
        my beginning and my end,
        my life, and, yes, my soul
and my heart bursts to tell you so

Discussion Guide

If you have used the guide for *Seniors in Love*, then you have discussed the meaning of the word "love" as well as issues arising from the loss of a former partner (death, divorce, etc.) and such questions as "Should I seek love again?" and "If I do, how do I behave?" *Seniors* took you through a series of steps in the love process, from deciding you could give and receive love again after your loss to finding someone to love and receiving that person's love in return.

One of the questions with which you dealt had to do with whether seniors love any differently than do junior and his sister. The superficial answer is "No," but with a subtle distinction: you have years of past experiences with which to deal, successes and failures which color your perspective.

In *The Greatest Companion* it assumed you have found that special person. You're in love and you're being loved. And it's wonderful!

But, and here's the burden of *Companion*: The hard work is just beginning. If you were married or in a partnership relationship earlier, you know (or if you don't know, you should) that maintaining the loving relationship is a full time job. Love must be proven each and every day.

What kind of love are we discussing?

Let's make it clear. We're talking about love, romance, amour. We're not talking merely about friendship or plutonic love; we're talking about passion and intimacy.

Questions:
1) Considering that love is an emotional/visceral response to someone, is there a difference between being in love when you're twenty and being in love when you're seventy?
2) If so, what are those differences and how do they manifest themselves, in you, in your partner?
3) What behavior is different?
4) Do expectations differ?

How is the book constructed?

The book is divided into twenty or more chapters, each dealing with a specific issue, each "essay" followed by one or more poems. It is hoped the poems will expand the ideas presented in the prose, enlarge the thoughts and say things the prose does not or cannot.

Using the poems are a risk the author has taken, since poetry is not as well considered as it once was. Yet life, and certainly love, beats with rhythms often best captured in the poetic word form.

Questions:
1) Is the poetry in the book a help or a hindrance?
2) If you could, would you write your own love poems?
3) Or is poetry so old fashioned that it's out of date?
4) Given that some of the poetry has been read, would you like to express yourself and your feelings so openly? Why/why not?

Where to begin?

Naturally it is hoped one begins with the introduction; it sets the stage and provides the atmosphere in which everything else follows.

Beyond that, since each chapter is independent, it's

pick and choose as the discussion group decides.

It's suggested that early attention be given to the chapter "The Fabric of Our Lives" if only because a new love relationship is the joining together of two separate and different persons and their lives.

Questions:
1) How difficult is (was) it to bring two people "of age" together, especially with their long past histories?
2) What compromises have to be made?
3) Probably most important of all, what was learned in earlier relationships that will impact the new?

Discussion groups and related themes.

When preparing this guide it's impossible to know if discussion of the book is to be a one time event or a series of events, thus, in consideration of time and interest, certain chapters of the book might be combined for discussion purposes. For example:

1) In any relationship words are vitally important. Several chapters deal with verbal (and silent) expressions of love. "K.I.S.S.," "Love Words," "So What is a Love Poem" might be considered together.

2) "Is it Sex or Love?," "Lovemaking Face to Face" and "On Cleaving" deal with the most intimate aspects of love.

3) "On Children," "Wealth and/or Love," "But What Makes a Love Poem?," and "Friends and Lovers" deal with some very practical concerns confronting the new partners.

4) The chapters on Adam and Eve and Tarzan and Jane have a tenuous relationship.

Lumping related chapters together is for the convenience of the discussion leader, and if there are but one or two discussion sessions, consolidating chapters is a necessary task.

Words and other expressions of love may or may not engender a lot of questions, and the matter of intimacy may be too delicate a matter for open discussion. Both are important and both give rise to obvious questions.

1) How does one verbally express oneself?
2) How does one physically express the tender closeness love implies?
3) And how does the other respond and similarly express the most intimate of emotions?
4) Will there be lovemaking on any mutual level?

The issues of children and money and friends by their very nature bring forth questions, and surely the discussion group can think of enough questions without prodding by the leader.

Point of view

The concept of body and soul as two separate entities is as old as recorded history; the concept produced plenty of philosophical and theological discussions and even led to prolonged wars as one or another social/political leader attempted to gain control over both another's body and soul.

Soul is used in *Companion* in the poetic sense, that is, having to do with one's spirit, and the individual is regarded as a unified whole, physical body and soul (spirit), no theological implication dividing the two.

But one's theology aside, there is a spirituality in the love relationship of significant meaning and of enormous proportions. Discussion group members may disagree, but *Companion* treats the love relationship as something holy and awesome and as near divinity as finite mortals can get. One might begin this discussion with the chapter "Love is Spiritual."

Questions:
1) Love is an emotion affecting the entire body. It begins in the brain and works its way into the stomach and into the muscles. Poetically, if not in reality, it strikes the heart. The heart does skip a beat and pounds loudly at the thought or sight of the one you love. Is such a picture real?
2) The initial flush of love's emotion quiets as time goes by. Is this an indication that love is diminishing or failing?
3) Does familiarity breed discontent?

Failure

The chance (and the risk) that one's love will end in failure is always present, so in the midst of learning (all over again) how to love, and maintaining that love, is a chapter on love's failure, "Do Not Open Unless Absolutely Necessary."

The point to remember is that if your love failed, love itself has neither failed nor died. Crushed you will be, your ego shattered, the light of your life gone dark. It happens and sometimes we never know why. There's no comfort in experiencing a failed love, only, perhaps, in knowing you tried your hardest to make it last.

Questions:
1) Have you been there?
2) How did you handle rejection?
3) How do you dismiss an unwanted partner?

5) Have you had second thoughts, either about rejection or being rejected?

6) Is it better to have loved and lost someone than never to have loved at all?

Finally, is love a myth?

Maybe this discussion should come earlier. There are those for whom love is an illusion, a myth, a falsehood even; at most a fairy tale. And there are those who wish to receive love but have no idea about how to give it. Worst, there are those who want to be loved but who for some reason refuse to give love. For all such persons, love doesn't exist, never did, never will. They simply cannot expand their lives enough to include another.

In spite of them, love is a reality with its mythic aspect, myth being the dreams of love, hopes realized, fears conquered, doubt vanquished. But we cannot live perpetually in the mythic state; we strive to make our myths come true, to find that person, that mate, that special one who lights our darkness and who brings color and beauty into our lives.

Being in love, our task is to make the myth, our dreams, real. It's not easy, but imagine the rewards. You give love, and miracle upon miracle, someone gives his or her love to you. Sounds good, doesn't it?

Questions:

1) Is such an outlook the province of the young only? Why or why not?

2) With all the experience of age, one's history of successes and failures, the "realities" of long life, does the senior have any right to perceive of love in terms of myth (dreams, hopes) coming true?

3) Has advanced age stilled the dream?

4) Is "young at heart" itself a myth?
5) Is one too old, too age-beaten, to experience love anew?

The senior asks numerous questions, not the least is whether he/she has any logical right to enjoy being in love again and whether for the senior love is just another word for convenience and overcoming loneliness. Thus,

7) Can there be passion role in senior love?
8) If there is, how is it acted out?

Complications

We cannot set the clock back by fifty years. We are what we are, elderly if not old, experienced but not innocent, tested by time if not always victorious. Love always is serious business, and the odds are the older one is the more serious it is. This may be one's final opportunity to achieve happiness with a loving partner. But the fundamental questions persists: should one seek and give love, can one justify whatever adjustments are required for a few short years of happiness, does one dare risk failure? These are personal questions; no one can answer for another

Did you enjoy *The Greatest Companion?*

Do you need more copies for friends and relatives? Of course you do! Order directly from the publisher at www.geroproducts.com, through your local bookstore, or use the order form below (may be photocopied).

Also, you may be interested in our other books and gifts:

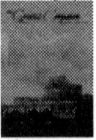

Qty —
The Greatest Companion: Reflections on Life, Love and Marriage After 60 by Robert Wolley - $19.95
Through prose and poetry, this book explores the joys of late-in-life love, provides reminders of what such a love needs to flourish, and reflects upon love's agelessness.

Qty —
Seniors in Love: A Second Chance for Single, Divorced and Widowed Seniors by Robert Wolley - $19.95
This well-reviewed book deals with the emotional, financial, physical, and other relevant issues facing seniors when considering a new, intimate relationship.

Qty —
ABC's for Seniors: Successful Aging Wisdom from an Outrageous Gerontologist by Ruth Jacobs - $19.95
In this book, Dr. Jacobs presents the essentials that enable a reader to harvest life fully for creative, healthy, successful, vigorous, and meaningful aging.

Qty —
Seniors in Love car magnet - $11.95
Show the world that love knows no age! An ideal wedding or anniversary gift! Measures six by four inches, in red, white, and gold. Removable. Fits any RV!

Qty __

"Golf is a good walk spoiled" mug - $9.95
Mark Twain said it, but it's as true today
as it was 100 years ago! Illustration and
quote, printed in black on both sides.

Qty __

"Grow old along with me" mug - $9.95
Robert Browning said it, but it's as true today
as it was 100 years ago! Illustration and
quote, printed in black on both sides. Truly,
"the best is yet to be"

Name _____

Address _____

City/State/Zip _____

Please mark the products you want, and their quantity
(Missouri residents only please add 5.25% sales tax).

There is no charge for shipping and handling, and all orders
are shipped from Greentop, Missouri (population 427).

Send check or money order to:
Hatala Geroproducts
PO Box 42
Greentop, MO 63546

www.ingramcontent.com/pod-product-compliance
Lightning Source LLC
Chambersburg PA
CBHW031508270326
41930CB00006B/307